The Dark Side of Nudges

The concept of "nudging" has hit news headlines in recent years following the implementation of nudge policies in many parts of the world, the establishment of behavioural policy units in some countries, and the award of the Nobel Prize in Economics to the behavioural economist Richard Thaler in 2017. However, questions remain about whether nudging is an optimal approach to policy-making.

This book presents a critical approach to the study of nudging to highlight the foundations, rationale and effects of current policy-making trends in the neoliberal age of behavioural economics.

In this provocative book, the author presents a re-examination of the methodological foundations of behavioural economics and its consequences for addressing the deep social and economic policy challenges of our times. It is argued that, although the concept of nudge proposed by Richard Thaler and Cass Sunstein rejects the theorization of economic behaviour under models of strict rationality, nudge policies focus on methodological individualism in economic thinking and economic policy.

The complexity of social and economic policy problems of the twenty-first century calls for a revision of our conceptual outlooks, and to increase recognition of the failure of methodological individualism in economics to address the unprecedented social, political, and environmental challenges of globalization. Offering a new take on the epistemological assumptions underlying behaviourally-informed policies, this book will prompt the general public to consider new ideas about the darker side of behavioural economics.

Maria Alejandra Madi, PhD, is currently director of The Green Economics Institute Academy (UK), researcher at the Centre for Pragmatism Studies (Brazil), and asssistant editor of the *International Journal of Pluralism and Economics Education*. She is a retired professor of economics at the Instituto de Economia, UNICAMP, Brazil.

Routledge Frontiers of Political Economy

257. The Economics of Military Spending
A Marxist Perspective
Adem Yavuz Elveren

258. Political Pluralism, Disagreement and Justice
The Case for Polycentric Democracy
Julian F. Müller

259. Nonviolent Political Economy
Theory and Applications
Edited by Freddy Cante and Wanda Tatiana Torres

260. Cognitive Capitalism, Welfare and Labour
The Commonfare Hypothesis
Andrea Fumagalli, Alfonso Giuliani, Stefano Lucarelli and Carlo Vercellone

261. Political Economy for Human Rights
Manuel Couret Branco

262. Alternative Approaches to Economic Theory
Complexity, Post Keynesian and Ecological Economics
Edited by Víctor A. Beker

263. The Dark Side of Nudges
Maria Alejandra Madi

For more information about this series, please visit: www.routledge.com/books/series/SE0345

The Dark Side of Nudges

Maria Alejandra Madi

Routledge
Taylor & Francis Group
LONDON AND NEW YORK

First published 2020
by Routledge
2 Park Square, Milton Park, Abingdon, Oxon OX14 4RN

and by Routledge
52 Vanderbilt Avenue, New York, NY 10017

Routledge is an imprint of the Taylor & Francis Group, an informa business

British Library Cataloguing in Publication Data
A catalogue record for this book is available from the British Library

Library of Congress Cataloging in Publication Data
A catalog record has been requested for this book

ISBN: 978-1-138-33862-3 (hbk)
ISBN: 978-0-429-44157-8 (ebk)

Typeset in Times New Roman
by Swales & Willis, Exeter, Devon, UK

To my daughters, Carolina and Fernanda, with love

Contents

Introduction: what does the "science" behind nudging really look like **1**

Why behavioural economics matters today 1

1 Setting the scene: the concept of nudge **7**

Introduction 7
What is wrong with the conventional model of rational choice? 8
Cognitive biases and choice heuristics 9
The choice architect 14
Improving decisions toward happiness 15
Conclusion 18

2 The nudge approach to policy making **23**

Introduction 23
The challenge of freedom 25
Information and incentives 33
Behavioural insights for policy change 37
Conclusion 41

3 Behavioural economics: methodological issues and philosophical concerns **46**

Introduction 46
The experimental setup 47
The ideal of rationality 53

Positive results and normative claims 58
Conclusion 59

4 Nudging citizens in the context of neoliberalism: their hidden side **64**

Introduction 64
Transformations in governmentality 65
Nudges and neoliberalism 70
Dark nudges 76
Digital nudges and surveillance 83
Conclusion 90

Conclusion **95**

Minds, markets, and economic policy in the neoliberal age 95

Index 102

Introduction

What does the "science" behind nudging really look like*

Why behavioural economics matters today

One of the most enduring fictional characters of all time first appeared on the scene in the late 1800s: the less well-known but influential *homo economicus*. The origins of the term *homo economicus* are somewhat obscure, meaning literally "economic man", and early references can be traced back to 1883, related to an economist from Oxford – S. Devas. His rational and maximizing behaviour quickly came to dominate economic theory. However, this theory of utility-maximizing rational choice does not focus on socio-economic systems' historically and geographically specific features.

In neoclassical theory, the rational choice approach considers the behaviour of individual decision-making units (individuals/firms) that are "representative" of a group, such as buyers or sellers in a given market. The environment where agents make choices is relevant to the identification of assumptions about their objectives, budget constraints, and decision rules. The basic idea is that, under prevailing circumstances, people face a known set of alternative choices and will choose the most preferred alternative among the available ones.[1] In this attempt, rational choices reveal utility maximization in a context where the solution of a constrained optimization problem is an adequate representation of what actually happens in decision-making in the real world. [2]

Almost a century after the emergence of *homo economicus*, behavioural economics developments in cognitive and social psychology criticize the rationality-maximizing assumption of the rational choice theory.[3] In this attempt, the psychologists Daniel Kahneman and Amos Tversky built a new approach to economics in the 1970s and 1980s. They challenged the assumption that individuals always make decisions based on self-interest. They advocate that, in real-life situations, emotional factors may influence

* I would specially like to thank Dr Stuart Birks, from the World Economics Association, for suggesting the title *The Dark Side of Nudges* for a short piece of writing on the topic in 2017.

human judgment and therefore, economic decisions. Individual behaviour is due to brains processing information in ways that are cognitively biased, that is to say, there is a systematic pattern of deviation in judgment or decision-making. Tversky and Kahneman (1981) used psychological evidence to show that human actions deviate from the rationality of *homo economicus* in all kinds of ways, since people make systematic errors of judgment that represent bias in relation to rational decisions. For instance, people value gains differently from former losses and value losses differently from former gains and these different valuations affect their current decisions.

Since the 1990s, other leaders in behavioural economics emerged, such as Dan Ariely, Robert Cialdini and Elke Weber, among others. The goal has been to study whether small interventions that don't cost much can change behaviour in large ways that serve both individuals and society. Their research results have been drawing strong interest from government leaders to transform policy making across job centres, schools, and local government offices. More recently, the integration of psychology to economics has been expanded through research projects that use computational rationality and artificial intelligence.

Looking back, the idea of behavioural government interventions was popularized in 2008 with the best seller *Nudge: Improving Decisions About Health, Wealth, and Happiness.* In the book, Richard Thaler and Cass Sunstein (2008) showed how this new understanding of human behaviour could have major consequences on policy making. As a matter of fact, the popularity of the concept of nudge grew after the publication of the book. According to Thaler and Sunstein (2008), a nudge refers to

> any aspect of the choice architecture that alters people's behaviour in a predictable way without forbidding any options or significantly changing their economic incentives. To count as a mere nudge, the intervention must be easy and cheap to avoid. Nudges are not mandates. Putting fruit at eye level counts as a nudge. Banning junk food does not.
>
> (p. 6)

In a previous paper, both researchers highlighted the paternalistic intention and the libertarian tone that overwhelm the concept. As a result, while policymakers shape contexts of individual choice toward optimal (cost-effective) policy goals, individuals are *free to choose* (Thaler and Sunstein 2003).

The aim of the nudge approach is both to experiment non-coercive alternatives to traditional regulation and to enhance cooperation between the public and the private sector. In the late 2000s, the Behavioural Insights Team – the Nudge Unit, as it is informally known – was created in the UK and many others countries – like Australia, Canada, the Netherlands, Germany, the United States, and Qatar – followed the behavioural policy recommendations. The Behavioural Insights Team in the UK explored and tested policy options by means of randomized controlled trials (RCTs) to pay taxes, for organ donation, and to stop smoking, among other examples.

At the core of nudging, there is the belief that:

- People do not always act in their own self-interest.
- People have biases and habits to be considered in the study of human behaviour to explain why people sometimes make choices that they themselves would consider poor.
- Small changes in how choices are presented can affect the way people can be steered toward better decisions

Nudging consumers is not new. This practice has been part of the communication and marketing strategies of advertisers and companies for decades. What is new today is that nudging has been spread as a communication tool within governments. Its rationality is supported by the principles of Libertarian Paternalism, as Thaler and Sunstein (2008) argue in their book *Nudge*. Their proposal enhances the use of nudges by governments to help citizens achieve small behavioural changes without coercion. The opt-out scheme makes it easier for people to be free to choose, that is to say, do what they actually want.

Taking into account this setting, the main concern is: why does nudging spread its influence on public policy? This book calls for a reflection on how influential behavioural economics has been in shaping public debate and policy. The focus on the normative implications of nudging certainly puts in question the realism of behavioural economics as economic theory.

Nudges are not trivial. Nudging is about exerting influence. It is time to deeply think about the dark side of nudging in order to find out how nudging relates to the age of neoliberal governance.

The general plan of the book

Today, there is a radical questioning of the whole matrix of economic knowledge in a context of unprecedented social, political, and environmental challenges. Indeed, the complexity of the social and economic problems of the twenty-first century calls to a revision, in a nontrivial way, of our conceptual outlooks.

While behavioural economics has received too much attention in contemporary debates, this book aims to develop a critical approach to the study of nudging in order to highlight the foundations, rationale, and effects of behavioural policies in the age of neoliberalism.

Although the concept of nudge rejects the theorization of economic knowledge under models of strict human rationality, its focus on individual behaviour turns out to reinforce methodological failures in economic thinking and economic policy.

Chapter 1 aims to present the conceptualization of nudge developed by Thaler and Sunstein. Behavioural economics' approach deviates from pure rationality since real people suffer from a variety of cognitive biases, including lack of self-control, excessive optimism, status quo bias, and susceptibility to framing of decisions, among others. Against the rational *homo economicus*, Thaler and Sunstein consider many false heuristics and biases that explain the gap between our good intentions and actual human behaviour. Then, human behaviour and choices exhibit bounded rationality, bounded self-interest, and bounded willpower.

At the centre of nudging is the behavioural economics' assumption that human behaviour and economic decisions are vulnerable to framing effects. Then nudges can be considered as social norms that can help people act rationally. And, as Thaler and Sunstein claim, the possibilities for nudges are everywhere.

Chapter 2 highlights the relation between nudges and Libertarian Paternalism. To understand the relevance of the meaning of Libertarian Paternalism, the concept deserves attention in historical and philosophical perspectives. In this attempt, Hayek´s rebirth of classical liberalism and the Libertarian Paternalism of Thaler and Sunstein are analysed. In accordance with Libertarian Paternalism, the role of public policy is to improve individual decision making since humans are predictably irrational in various ways. Nudging tries to help people increase their level of subjective welfare, something they cannot do by themselves due to cognitive biases. In this attempt, Libertarian Paternalism maximally preserves the freedom of choice while the government interventions frame choices, leaving the final decisions to individuals. The chapter also points out the spread of behavioural polios in major policy agendas, in particular through strengthening the information and incentives available to people make better choices.

Chapter 3 states that through the transportation of control trials' results to policy contexts, behavioural economics has spread normative recommendations to make people "happier" as the result of government interventions (nudges) that can help people change their behaviours and act rationally. As this chapter argues, the normative programme of Libertarian Paternalism is built upon methodological foundations that raise interrelated questions: how reliable are empirical data underlying its normative conclusions? How convincing is its theoretical justification for government intervention? Despite the non-uniformity of population, the normative recommendations of behavioural economics are applicable by default to the entire society. This applicability is justified by the principles of Libertarian Paternalism where government interventions impose almost no costs on rational individuals and preserve their freedom of choice. The main concern is whether economic policy should be built upon observations in control trials and what surreptitious issues should be considered. In our view, behavioural economics does not dismiss the Cartesian narrative and the norm of rationality that have been rejected by Friedrich Nietzsche and Michel Foucault, among others, in the last centuries. Relying on Foucault′s analysis of the role of normalization in modern societies, this chapter addresses that nudges are at heart of the techniques of modern power.

Chapter 4 argues that the processes of market deregulation, privatization, financialization of corporate strategies, and labour flexibility can be associated with the Libertarian Paternalist governance. Indeed, the spread of use of nudging by governments is at the core of a set of complex economic, social, and political interrelations. More specifically, the chapter explores how the articulation between Libertarian Paternalism and the neoliberal policy interventions turns out to shape the individual behaviour in the markets. Shedding light on the contributions of Jeremy Bentham's Panopticon and Foucault's biopolitics, this chapter illuminates a vast set of issues related to the outcomes of "soft" government interventions and power techniques. Current governmentality challenges enhance a deep reflection on the neoliberal self-governance of nudging. This scenario also raises economic, social, and political concerns about technocracy and surveillance. In what follows, we shall be concerned with the following questions: Can digital nudging be qualified as Libertarian Paternalism? Are the conceptualization and current practice of nudging appropriate for building a democratic society?

Notes

1 If the number of possible alternative choices is infinite, it may not be possible to represent the preference relation with a utility function. In the model of rational choice, preferences are represented by a utility function – a mathematical function – only if the relationship satisfies completeness and transitivity.

2 It is possible that a model might have no equilibrium or more than one equilibrium.

3 In the last decades, psychological science has experienced an increasing integration with other scientific disciplines. Behavioural economics is underscored in

the sub-discipline of neuroeconomics, which uses neural imaging to identify which areas of the brain become active during particular tasks.

References

Thaler, R. and Sunstein, C. (2003). Libertarian paternalism. *American Economic Review*, 93 (2): 175–179.

Thaler, R. and Sunstein, C. (2008). *Nudge: Improving Decisions about Health, Wealth, and Happiness*. New Haven: Yale University Press.

Tversky, A. and Kahneman, D. (1981). The framing of decisions and the psychology of choice. *Science*, 211 (4481): 453–458.

1 Setting the scene

The concept of nudge

Introduction

Behavioural economics aims at deconstructing the "standard" rational choice approach to decision-making based on utility-maximizing principles given constraints determined by prices, income, and available information.

The behavioural economics approach argues that human behaviour is characterized by cognitive biases, lack of willpower, and selfishness, which prevent making rational choices. Optimal (rational) economic behaviour can also be affected by:

1) the way in which information is processed to make choices;
2) how choices are framed and attended to; and
3) how unobservable mental states take part in the decision-making.

Therefore, behavioural economics turns out to be in close affinity with cognitive psychology, which has been developed in direct opposition to "classical" behaviourism (Lambert 2006, 52).

The concern about the challenges to rational behaviour is not new. Classical behaviourism – a leading school of twentieth century psychology associated with the name of J. Watson – assumed that only actually observed or objectively measurable behaviour can serve as the subject matter for psychology (Angner and Loewenstein 2007). However, the predecessors to behavioural economics are mainly associated with the ideas of Herbert Simon who was awarded the Nobel Prize in 1978. Simon (1987) put into question the rational choice assumptions and coined the term "bounded rationality". His conceptualization of rationality refers to the entire spectrum of constraints on human knowledge and capabilities that prevent people from behaving as predicted by neoclassical theory.[1] Bounded rationality refers to human decisions bounded by limitations in both knowledge and computational capacity.

The recent behavioural turn in economic theory is considered to have been triggered by papers published by Tversky and Kahneman (1973; 1974). After criticizing the orthodox expected utility theory, the authors offered an alternative concept for decision making under uncertainty that was called "prospect theory". Thaler's (1980; 1985) relevant contributions appeared at the same time and provided a great deal of empirical evidence on the "suboptimality" of decisions made by economic agents, such as underestimating opportunity costs, the inability to abstract from sunk costs, and insufficient self-control. Thaler, like Kahneman and Tversky, aimed to develop an empirically adequate theory of choice that would be able to describe actually observed decision-making processes.[2]

All things considered, Thaler and Sunstein's research on nudges refers to a variety of simple changes in the choice environment. Nudging is supposed to work by appealing to individual cognitive biases in decision-making.

What is wrong with the conventional model of rational choice?

The neoclassical approach to economic theory presupposes perfect rationality of the economic agents. Economists mean several things when referring to "perfect rationality" Camerer et al. (2003, 1214–1215). First, individuals have well-ordered preferences (objectives) and aim at fully satisfying them when making decisions. Second, they do not make mistakes (at least systematically) when calculating the benefits and costs associated with multiple choices. Third, in uncertain situations they can make probabilistic estimates of potential outcomes using all available information and revise those estimates as soon as new data arrives. Obviously, the first point is the most important.

This concept of rationality is purely formal and rationality turns out to be a synonym for a consistency of preferences that are manifested in the actual choices made by an individual. According to Arrow (1996, xiii), "the major meaning of rationality is a condition of consistency among choices made from different sets of alternatives". In this approach, given a certain order of preferences and a certain set of constraints (physical, institutional, informational) individuals choose the best options of those available to them. As a result, it is expected that whatever choice they make, they will have no reasons to regret them or take them back (Saint-Paul 2011).

The *homo economicus* has only one utility function, that is to say, a single set of preferences. This principle is the starting point for the neoclassical normative approach to welfare economics that interprets the welfare of a society as an aggregate of individual preferences (Sugden 2008).

Tversky and Kahneman (1986) analysed the formal requirements to be met by choices. Among the axioms of the rational choice theory, two appear to be the most significant: transitivity and context-independence.

- The condition of transitivity assumes that, if A is preferred over B, and B is preferred over C, then A is preferred over C. Rational agents can make choices when presented not only with isolated pairs of alternatives but also with multiple options.
- The context-independence condition assumes that a choice between two options is independent from the order in which they are offered. Adding a new option to the existing two should not influence the choice unless the third option is preferable to the previous two. To sum up, the results of rational choices do not depend on how the options are presented.

Against the neoclassical theory assumptions on human behaviour, where human beings are rational decision-makers that act towards self-interest, behavioural economists developed some critical ideas:

- First, as Tversky and Kahneman (1986, 252) state, empirical research showed that in real life "deviations of actual behavior from the normative model [of rational choice] are too widespread to be ignored, too systematic to be dismissed as random error, and too fundamental to be accommodated by relaxing the normative system".
- Second, irrational behaviour undermines the belief of a single rational self. In fact, there are two selves, but only one makes rational decisions.
- Third, the normative prescriptions of the rational choice theory are undermined since:
  - i) people have a poor understanding of their own true interests and often act contrary to them; and
  - ii) the options actually chosen by individuals could not be the best for them out of all of those available.

Cognitive biases and choice heuristics

It is undeniable that how the human mind works is one of the greatest contemporary debates. Behavioral economics rejects the assumption of pure rationality in order to explain why real people suffer from a variety of cognitive biases that affect their decision-making and wellbeing, including lack of self-control, and excessive optimism, among others. Indeed, Thaler and Sunstein advocated the need to consider the assumption of bounded rationality in the attempt to understand human actions and to analyse the heurisitcs and biases that explain the gap between our good intentions and our actual behaviour.

Resting on the foundational scholarship of Kahneman and Tversky, Thaler and Sunstein address that people often operate under the influence of systematic cognitive biases that prevent them from making sound decisions. Indeed, the changing paradigm in understanding human behaviour started in the early 1970s, under the research of Kahneman. He believes that the distinction between "*econs*" and "*humans*" (while *econs* refer to the rational *homo economicus*, *humans* suffer from a variety of cognitive biases that prevent them from being fully rational) contrasts the traditional conception related to the neo-classical rational behaviour with many insights emerging from cognitive psychology.[3] Since the late 1970s and throughout the 1980s, Kahneman developed his investigations and highlighted the cognitive biases. For instance, his research results criticized the neoclassical theory of consumer rationality, the relevance of loss aversion, and the life-cycle hypothesis. The research results put into question the neoclassical assumption of self-control and the application of the concept of opportunity cost in economic decisions that permeate the relationship between present goods and future goods. Kahneman stated that *humans* do not have self-control. In addition, he identified two types of *human*: planners, who think and care about the future, and doers, who do not.

In the book *Misbehaving*, Thaler (2015) explains that, between 1986 and 1994, the debate within the Chicago school of economics was marked by resistance towards the new ideas. However, the research and the training of researchers continued to be focused on the identification of financial market anomalies and criticism of the efficient markets hypothesis, the consumer sovereignty, and the transaction cost hypothesis of Ronald Coase. Since then, research on cognitive biases has been close to neuroscience and neuroeconomics.

Kahneman, Tversky, and different specialists on behavioural economics, built up a research programme that focuses on judgment under uncertainty. Among the fundamental outcomes, they recognized errors in probabilistic thinking. In Tversky and Kahneman's (1973, 237) claim the following:

> In making expectations and decisions under vulnerability, individuals don't seem to pursue the analytics of possibility or the factual hypothesis of forecast. Rather, they depend on a predetermined number of heuristics which once in a while yield sensible decisions and at times lead to serious and efficient blunders.

Thaler and Sunstein's research relies on the Dual Process Cognitive Theories (DPTs), especially as portrayed by Kahneman. The human brain functions in ways that invite a distinction between two kinds of thinking: automatic thinking and reflective (rational) thinking. Kahneman called these ways of thinking System 1 and System 2, respectively. Automatic thinking is characterized by being fast and intuitive. Reflective thinking refers to the processing of information in a deliberate and conscious way. Therefore, it is slow and demands effort and concentration.

System 1 plays a very important role in decision making, particularly in the case of making judgments under the circumstances of ambiguity, limitation of time, and thought processes. System 2 is under control, intentional, purposeful, and based on analysis. For instance, people make long-term plans for saving or dieting (utilising System 2), but then, when the time comes, reverse those plans and fail to resist to the desire for short-term gratification (employing System 1). Moreover, making different choices can reveal different emotional states, despite prices and levels of income. In summary, DPTs explain why human beings not only fall short of rational decision-making, but their behaviour may actually systematically deviate from its normative prescriptions.[4]

The empirical systematic errors in reasoning and judgment have been named "cognitive illusions". Among the constraints on rational decision-making, the researchers highlight the limited ability of individuals:

1) to allocate their attention to more than a comparatively small number of relevant features in their environment; and
2) to assign probabilities and appropriate weights to a variety of threats and opportunities.[5]

Tversky and Kahneman (1991) also noted the susceptibility of human beings to the influence of the manner in which their choices are framed. In other words, the framing might dominate the subsequent choice, since this framing provokes differing perceptions of risk.[6]

In view of the empirical research, Thaler and Sunstein (2008) also favour the understanding of flaws in human behaviour that frequently lead to short-sightedness in decision making:

- the *present bias* that refers to a tendency with regard to economic decisions that involves time discounting;
- the *availability bias* that refers to the influence of the tendency to perceive circumstances that are easily remembered;

- the *confirmation bias* that refers to a tendency to accommodate new information within the existing set of beliefs that might lead to over-confidence;
- the *status quo bias* that refers to the tendency for individuals to continue to make the same choice even after the decision has lost all or part of its benefit; and
- the *context-dependence bias* that refers to the influence of the formal characteristics of the frame on decisions.

A cognitive bias is considered to be systematic "deviation" in the outcomes of the decisions people make and they arise from the application of one or more heuristics. These heuristics are "rules of thumb" used to make decisions or judgments (Thaler and Sunstein 2008, 22).[7]

In the light of the choice heuristics, Kahneman and Frederick (2002, 53) state:

> We will say that judgment is mediated by a heuristic when an individual assesses a specified target attribute of a judgment object by substituting another property of that object – the heuristic attribute – which comes more readily to mind.

Table 1.1 summarizes some of the main choice heuristics that can affect human judgment under uncertainty.

Table 1.1 Behavioural economics: main choice heuristics

Choice heuristic	*Correlated tendency in human behaviour*
Anchoring-and-adjustment	A sequence of judgments and decisions are influenced by the interpretation of future information using an initial piece of information as an anchor.
Availability	Current judgments and decisions are based on information held in memory.
Representativeness	Current judgments and decisions consider as relevant the information about the similarity of other events.
Sunk cost fallacy	People make choices oriented to avoiding losses rather than acquiring gains.
Familiarity	Past choices are considered in new situations and, therefore, past behaviours influence current behaviours.
Naive diversification	The search for a larger variety of choices occurs when individuals have to make simultaneous choices.

Source: Tversky and Kahneman (1974); Benartzi and Thaler (2001).

Taking into account this theoretical background, behavioural economics' empirical programme has been oriented to identify the "anomalies". In this respect, Mario J. Rizzo and Douglas Glen Whitman (2009, 951) highlight that the variety of deviations from the rational human being is large and constantly growing. A small sample of the most important "anomalies" is presented below:

- *Hyperbolic discounting.* In real life many (maybe even most) people act as inconsistent "discounters" since the discount rates they use rather increase as the compared periods come closer to the present moment.[8] For example, due to insufficient self-control, an individual may plan to start saving for retirement or a strict diet, but they will abandon these ideas when the next year arrives. Indeed, excessive impatience (high, short-term discount rate) might also motivate people to make decisions with immediate benefits and delayed costs. Therefore, hyperbolic discounting may be the reason for phenomena such as addictive behaviour (e.g., towards drugs or food), regular postponement of important decisions, building portfolios containing incompatible financial instruments (e.g., using high-interest credit cards while at the same time buying low-interest securities), excessive borrowing, or low saving rates. Hyperbolic discounting may be considered evidence of conflict between the two selves, each with its own special utility function: one impatient and only concerned with the present, the other prudent and future-oriented. The conflict between the selves leads to inconsistent behaviour.
- *"Cold" and "hot" psychological states.* The current emotional states may have a decisive influence on choices. While the feelings of anger, fear, admiration, and excitement (the so called hot states) may lead to spontaneous decisions, rational thought (the so called cold state), may lead to well-measured decisions. Reacting suboptimally, people may overestimate short-term benefits and underestimate the long-term costs of a given decision. Emotional states also reveal the conflict between the two selves.
- *Errors of optimism and pessimism.* Errors of optimism (or the underestimation of the probability of undesirable events) make individuals self-confident and take more risks in their decisions. For instance, investors generally underestimate their own chances of losses in high-risk financial assets. Errors of pessimism make people lose self-confidence and this leads to strong risk aversion because they overestimate the probability of undesirable events.[9]

What behavioural economics emphasizes is that, as the result of heuristics and cognitive biases, people make choices that are inconsistent with their best own interests. In this conceptualization, there is the recognition of systematic deviations from a standard of comparison. Tversky and Kahneman (1983, 311) state:

> Studies of reasoning and problem solving have shown that people often fail to understand or apply an abstract logical principle even when they can use it properly in concrete familiar contexts..

The cognitive biases turned out to be "behavioural market failures" (Sunstein 2014). And the standard of comparison is the *homo economicus* who still stands at the centre of the mainstream economic theory.

The choice architect

In the middle 1980s, Kahneman's research results on the analysis of consumer behaviour and its relation to prices pointed out that the perception of fairness depends on the endowment effect and the status quo. In other words, noticed and unnoticed features of the environment may influence their decisions.

What behavioural economics explores in the analysis of human behaviour and economic decisions is that *humans* are vulnerable to framing effects. People tend to take the description of a situation as fixed, without reformulating it in different ways. Then, the principal tools of nudging, or of "choice architecture", as Sunstein and Thaler call it, are the provision of various types of information to choosers, and the selection of "default rule decision" frames. They coined the term "choice architect" to describe the person who is responsible for designing the framework for decision-making and implementing the nudges.

Thaler and Sunstein (2003, 1190–1195) provide a series of guidelines for the choice architects to operate. The first step is to examine the full costs and benefits of the possible design frameworks.

However, in many cases, as a cost-benefit analysis will not be warranted or possible, they highlighted several rules of thumb. The default rule would be the choice that the majority would select if all explicit choices were revealed. Thaler and Sunstein (2008) advise the choice architect to expect error. As they realized that the one-size-fits-all solutions may not fit, they have included an opt-out option. Given that the problem of choice architecture is unavoidable, the advocates of nudges argue that the opt-out is a reasonable solution (Jolls and Sunstein 2006). Therefore, in light of the potential pitfalls, the choice architecture should select the choice that fewer people opt out of as default.[10] The authors also provide broad principles to guide the choice architect:

- default rules are relevant;
- complex choices should be structured in manageable ways;
- incentives matter; and
- behavioural errors should be systematically expected.

If the choice architect can design the decision frameworks in accordance with these guidelines and principles, people can be "nudged" into better lifestyles. The purpose of nudging is to help people make better choices as judged by themselves. The philosophy of nudging has been referred to as Libertarian Paternalism and its principles are going to be analysed in the next chapter.

Improving decisions toward happiness

Arthur Pigou, the father of welfare economics, analysed the conditions that prevent perfect markets to guarantee the maximization of benefits for all society. The foundations of welfare are the individual's satisfactions or utilities. Individual economic welfare refers to the satisfaction or utility that an individual gets from his expenditure on goods and services. As Pigou claims, social welfare is considered as the sum of all individual welfares of society (Madi 2017).

Indeed, his analysis placed welfare at the centre of the discipline of economics. In the book *Wealth and Welfare* (1912), Pigou concludes that improved economic welfare would result from an increase in national income, an increase in the absolute share of national income that goes to poor people, and a reduction in the variability of national income and, in particular, of the share of national income received by poor people.

Pigou developed these ideas in *The Economics of Welfare* that was first published in 1920. In this book, Pigou highlighted that economic welfare will not be maximized if there is a divergence between the marginal net social product and marginal private net product of economic activities. He also clarified that the concept of externalities refers to benefits (positive externalities) or costs (negative externalities) imposed on others that are not considered by the economic agents in their decisions. In view of these externalities, Pigou suggested taxes or subsidies– the so called Pigouvian taxes and subsidies.

Negative or positive externalities in production justify government intervention. If economic activities create a negative externality – such as degradation of the environment – a tax should be imposed on this activity to discourage it. Moreover, if economic activities create positive externalities – such as the promotion of higher levels of education – subsidies should be granted. In other words, Pigou advocated government interventions to introduce compensation mechanisms in the markets through taxes or subsidies. Years later, Lionel Robbins (1938) challenged this normative approach to welfare economics because he thought it was based on the assumption that utility is measurable. Moreover, in the 1960, Ronald Coase put into question the efficacy of the Pigouvian taxes and subsidies because governments fail as markets do.

More recently, the spread of behavioural economics has been associated with a discussion about preferences and welfare. Against rational choice theory, behavioural economics shows that preferences are not always transitive; they are context-dependent and not stable. In this theoretical background, individual preferences involve alternatives of choice and their order depends on the expected levels of subjective utility.[11] Hausman (2012) argues that the characterization of economic preferences as subjective comparative evaluations relies on the four axioms of ordinal utility theory that constitute the core of neoclassical economics (and rational theory). There is a ranking of complete, transitive, and context-independent alternatives and such a ranking results from a subjective comparative evaluation among the alternatives. In rational choice theory, the axiom of completeness implies that economic agents evaluate alternatives in a comparative way; the axiom of transitivity requires that economic agents carefully and evaluate all alternatives; the axiom of context-independence emerges only if thee economic agents evaluate everything that matters to them to make the decisions; while the axiom choice determination implies that preferences are not just judgments but involve action. Another important assumption of rational choice theory is the stability of preferences.[12]

In the article *Social Norms and Social Roles*, Sunstein (1996, 4) says that individual rationality, behaviour, and choices are a function of social norms, social meanings, and social roles. What is rational for an agent is a function of, and mediated by, social roles and associated norms. However, what lies behind choices is a set of things – aspirations, values, physical states, reactions to existing roles and norms, judgments, emotions, and beliefs. Then, the interaction of these forces may produce different outcomes in accordance with the particular contexts. Therefore, individual preferences are not aprioristic and choices have a contextual nature. In his view, what lies behind a choice is a particular setting and a choice does not suggest a contextual valuation of social goods.

Sunstein also refers to the unavoidable management of norms as an instrument of legal policy since changes in social norms might improve social well-being. The management of social norms by the government moves norms toward the increase of the individual benefits or the decrease of the individual costs associated with certain actions.

In fact, social norms can operate as taxes or as subsidies that aim to change individual behaviour. In his view, social norms and judgments about the benefits and costs of individual actions are difficult to separate.

The government has many different tools for the management of social norms:

- The government may restrict itself to education.
- The government may persuade people to change attitudes and choices rather than simply to offer information to influence the choice.
- The government may use economic instruments to tax or subsidize choices. Alcoholic drinks, tobacco products, generation of waste, and some polluting activities are met with taxes (though some of these choices are subsidized too).
- The government may impose restrictions, such as banning smoking in public spaces.
- The government action can refer to straightforward coercion that entirely forecloses choice.

Indeed, some government interventions can be mildly intrusive while others may foreclose choice. In the book *Nudge*, Thaler and Sunstein (2008, 6) define a nudge as follows:

> A nudge, as we will use the term, is any aspect of the choice architecture that alters people's behaviour in a predictable way without forbidding any options or significantly changing their economic incentives. To count as a mere nudge, the intervention must be easy and cheap to avoid. Nudges are not mandates. Putting fruit at eye level counts as a nudge. Banning junk food does not.

Nudges are social norms that can help people act rationally. Thaler and Sunstein claim that the possibilities for nudges are everywhere. The classical example of a cafeteria that lays out food in a way that encourages people to select carrot sticks over French fries or dessert is appropriated to show the benefit of educating consumers about what is in their own best interest without restricting choice.[13]

A central feature of Libertarian Paternalism is that nudges improve decisions as judged by people's own preferences and not by the bureaucracy (Thaler and Sunstein 2008, 10). When designing social norms, the choice architect may consider three categories of nudges and their effects on individual welfare, as judged by the individuals themselves:

- Some nudges help individuals satisfy consumer preferences, mainly by enabling people to satisfy their own preferences.
- Other nudges help people overcome the lack of self-control of individuals and help people to make choices consistent with them, as judged by themselves (AJBT) criterion.
- Some nudges alter people's preferences and, in this case, the AJBT criterion may be more difficult to operationalize since there is not a unique solution.

Although the AJBT criterion restricts the universe of solutions, it guides the choice architects to design consumer preferences and opportunity costs.[14]

Following behavioural interventions, many governments have already started the application of the results of psychological research to influence people's behaviour. What is behind the new science of well-being (and nudging), is that higher well-being is not related to growing income or expansion of employment, but to behavioural changes of individuals toward rational decisions.

Relying on control trials designed by experimental governments, the normativity of Libertarian Paternalism reverts into "small" interventions. The leader of the Nudge Unit in the UK, David Halpern (2015, 291) states that idea of "radical incrementalism" is behind the success of this normative approach that aims to apply the radical incrementalism principle in public policy. There is the belief that this principle can support transformative and cost-effectiveness policies. In his view, improvements in rational judgment and well-being can be achieved by systematically testing small variations in everything people do. Therefore, policy makers should actively experiment with "what works", and evaluate and iterate the effective results. In this scenario, nudging people turns out to be an experimental approach to policy making, and the increasing use of modem statistics by governments is a related phenomenon.

Conclusion

Behavioural economics states that real people suffer from a variety of cognitive biases, including lack of self-control, excessive optimism, status quo bias, and susceptibility to framing of decisions, among others.

Against the rational *homo economicus*, Thaler and Sunstein search for explanations of the gap between human intentions and actual behavior since choices exhibit bounded rationality, bounded self-interest, and limited willpower. What behavioural economics highlights is that economic decisions are vulnerable to framing effects. Thaler and Sunstein claim that the possibilities for nudges are everywhere and people need help to make rational choices and improve their well-being. The governments need to find out "what works" to improve individuals' well-being.

Notes

1 Katona appears to have been the first who started to use the term "behavioral economics" (Katona 1951).On the developments of the "old behavioural" approach see Sent (2004).
2 In this new research scenario, we can also highlight distinguished scholars such as G. Akerlof, D. Ariely, C. Camerer, G. Loewenstein, D. Laibson, T. O'Donohue, M. Rabin, K. Sunstein, and A. Shleifer. Some commentators consider behavioural economics as a true revolution in modern economic thought (Costa-Font 2011).
3 The development of behavioral law and economics (BL&E) in policy relevant debates has been substantial (Wright and Ginsburg 2012).
4 For a complete explanation of how Systems 1 and Systems 2 work, see Daniel Kahneman's (2011) well-known book *Thinking, Fast and Slow.*
5 On the heuristics biases programme see Kahneman et al. (1982), Tversky and Kahneman (1974) and (Tversky and Kahneman 1983).
6 On the cognitive biases see Kahneman (2003) and Sunstein (2013)
7 For a discussion on heuristics, see Lockton (2012).
8 The neoclassical analysis of intertemporal choice builds upon the fact that individuals prefer present goods to future ones. They are willing to exchange present goods for future goods at a discount rate that can be considered the measure of the "sacrifice". Those who are patient would require a low discount rate to exchange present for future goods. However, those who are very impatient would require a high discount rate. See Laibson (1997).
9 For a discussion on the behavioural market failures see Camerer et al. (2003).
10 See Glod (2015) on a critical approach to how nudges often fail to treat people according to their own preferences.
11 See Arrow (1958) on an anlysis of utilities, attitudes, and choices.
12 For a debate on normative issues in welfare economics and nudging see Hausman (2012) in addition to Hausman and Welch (2010).
13 Other examples of nudging can be found in Thaler and Sunstein (2008, 229–235). For a list of favourites from the book, see https://nudges.files.wordpress.com/2008/04/our-dozen-nudges1.pdf
14 On this topic, see the analyiss of Berg and Davidson (2017) on behavioural policy making.

References

Angner, E. and Loewenstein, G. F. (2007). Behavioral economics. In U. Mäki (Ed.), *Book Review. Handbook of the Philosophy of Science: Philosophy of Economic*. Amsterdam: Elsevier. pp. 641–690. 2012. Available at SSRN: https://ssrn.com/abstract=957148

Arrow, K. (1958). Utilities, attitudes, choices: A review note. *Econometrica*, 26 (1): 1–23.

Arrow, K. J. (1996). Preface. In J. K. Arrow, E. Colombatto, and M. Perlman (Eds.), *The Rational Foundations of Economic Behaviour*. London: Macmillan. pp. xiii–xvii.

Benartzi, S. and Thaler, R. (2001). Naïve diversification strategies in defined contribution saving plans. *American Economic Review*, 91: 79–98.

Berg, C. and Davidson, S. (2017). Behavioral policy and its stakeholders nudging, calculation, and utopia. *Journal of Behavioral Economics for Policy*, (1): 49–52. Special Issue. Available at: https://sabeconomics.org/journal/RePEc/beh/JBEPv1/articles/JBEP-1-S-9.pdf

Camerer, C., Issacharoff, S., Loewenstein, G., O'Donoghue, T., and Rabin, M. (2003). Regulation for conservatives: Behavioral economics and the case for "asymmetric paternalism". *University of Pennsylvania Law Review*, 151 (1): 1211–1254.

Coase, R. H. (1960). The problem of social cost. *Journal of Law and Economics*, 3: 1–44.

Costa-Font, J. (2011). Behavioural welfare economics: Does "behavioural optimality" matter? *CESifo Economic Studies*, 57 (4): 551–559.

Glod, W. (2015). How nudges often fail to treat people according to their own preferences. *Social Theory and Practice*, 41 (4): 599–617. Special Issue: Preference, Choice, and (Libertarian) Paternalism. October.

Halpern, D. (2015). *Inside the Nudge Unit: How Small Changes can Make a Big Difference*. London: WH Allen.

Hausman, D. M. (2012). *Preference, Value, Choice, and Welfare*. Cambridge; New York: Cambridge University Press.

Hausman, D. M. and Welch, B. (2010). Debate: To nudge or not to nudge. *Journal of Political Philosophy*, 18 (1): 123–136.

Jolls, C. and Sunstein, C. (2006). Debiasing through law. *Journal of Legal Studies*, 35: 199–241.

Kahneman, D. (2003). Maps of bounded rationality: Psychology for behavioral economics. *American Economic Review*, 93 (5): 1449–1475.

Kahneman, D. (2011). *Thinking, Fast and Slow*. New York: Farrar, Straus and Giroux.

Kahneman, D. and Frederick, S. (2002). Representativeness revisited: Attribute substitution in intuitive judgment. In T. Gilovich, D. Griffin, and D. Kahneman (Eds.), *Heuristics and Biases: The Psychology of Intuitive Judgment*. London: Cambridge University Press. pp. 49–81.

Kahneman, D., Slovik, P., and Tversky, A. (Eds.) (1982). *Judgment under Uncertainty: Heuristics and Biases*. Cambridge: Cambridge University Press.

Kahneman, D. and Tversky, A. (1979). Prospect theory: An analysis of decision under risk. *Econometrica*, 47 (2): 263–291.

Katona, G. (1951). *Psychological Analysis of Economic Behavior*. New York: McGraw-Hill.

Laibson, D. (1997). Golden eggs and hyperbolic discounting. *Quarterly Journal of Economics*, 112 (2): 443–477.

Lambert, C. (2006). The marketplace of perceptions. *Harvard Magazine*, 2: 50–95.

Lockton, D. (2012). Cognitive biases, heuristics and decision-making in design for behaviour change. Working Paper. Available at: http://danlockton.co.uk

Madi, M. A. C. (2017). *Pluralist Readings in Economcis: Key-Concepts and Policy Tools for the 21st Century*. Sharjah, U.A.E.: Bentham Publishers.

Pigou, A. C. (1912). *Wealth and Welfare*. London: Macmillan.

Pigou, A. C. (1920). *The Economics of Welfare*. London: Macmillan.

Rizzo, M. J. and Whitman, D. G. (2009). The knowledge problem of the new paternalism. *Brigham Young University Law Review*, 4: 905–968.

Robbins, L. (1938). Interpersonal comparisons of utility. *Economic Journal*, 48 (192): 635–641.

Saint-Paul, J. (2011). *The Tyranny of Utility. Behavioral Social Science and the Role of Paternalism*. Princeton: Princeton University Press.

Sent, E.-M. (2004). Behavioral economics: How psychology made its (limited) way back into economics. *History of Political Economy*, 36 (4): 735–760.

Simon, H. A. (1987). Bounded rationality. In J. Eatwell, M. Milgate, and P. Newman (Eds.), *Utilility and Probability: The New Palgrave Book Series*. New York: W.W. Norton. pp.15–18.

Sugden, R. (2008). Why incoherent preferences do not justify paternalism. *Constitutional Political Economy*, 19 (3): 226–248.

Sunstein, C. (1996). Social norms and social roles. *Columbia Law Review*, 96 (4): 903–968.

Sunstein, C. (2013). The storrs lectures: Behavioral economics and paternalism. *Yale Law School*, 122: 1828–1899.

Sunstein, C. (2014). *Why Nudge? The Politics of Libertarian Paternalism*. New Haven: Yale University Press.

Thaler, R. H. (2015). *Misbehaving: How Economics Became Behavioural*. London: Allen Lane.

Thaler, R. (1980). Toward a positive theory of consumer choice. *Journal of Economic Behavior and Organization*, 1 (1): 39–60.

Thaler, R. (1985). Mental accounting and consumer choice. *Marketing Science*, 4 (1): 199–214.

Thaler, R. and Sunstein, C. (2003). Libertarian paternalism is not an oxymoron. *University of Chicago Law Review*, 70 (4): 1159–1202.

Thaler, R. and Sunstein, C. (2008). *Nudge: Improving Decisions about Health, Wealth, and Happiness*. New Haven: Yale University Press.

Tversky, A. and Kahneman, D. (1973). Availability: A heuristic for judging frequency and probability. *Cognitive Psychology*, 5 (2): 207–232.

Tversky, A. and Kahneman, D. (1974). Judgment under uncertainty: Heuristics and biases. *Science*. New Series, 185 (4157): 1124–1131.

Tversky, A. and Kahneman, D. (1983). Extensional versus intuitive reasoning: The conjunction fallacy in probability judgment. *Psychological Review*, 90 (4): 293–315.

Tversky, A. and Kahneman, D. (1986). Rational choice and the framing of decisions. *Journal of Business*, 59 (4, Pt. 2): S251–S278.

Tversky, A. and Kahneman, D. (1991). Loss aversion in riskless choice: A reference-dependent model. *The Quarterly Journal of Eco*nomics, 106 (4): 1039–1061.

Wright, J. D. and Ginsburg, D. H. (2012). Behavioural law and economics: Its origins, fatal flaws, and implications for liberty. *Northwestern University Law Review*, 106: 1033–1088.

2 The nudge approach to policy making

Introduction

Economics has changed significantly since the 1970s. This process involved an evolving relationship between economic theory and applied economics, with consequent transformations in the way economics is itself conceived.[1] Taking into account this background, the development of behavioural economics can be considered as part of the process of development of applied economics after the 1970s where some new theories were welcomed for their renewed understanding of economic behaviour, bringing in imperfect information or psychological evidence.

In this context: *how has the rise of behavioural economics affected the way economists have conceived rationality, economics methodology, and policy making?*[2]

In order to demonstrate the existence of cognitive biases and the failings of neo-classical rationality, behavioural economists rely on empirical data, collected through designed experiments and surveys. From the point of view of positive analysis, its most important message is the rejection of the commonly accepted model of rational choice that has traditionally provided the behavioural foundation for the greater part of contemporary economic theory (Kapeliushnikov 2015).

Behavioural economists go beyond positive analysis and proceed to develop normative recommendations for governments. The normative programme, built upon the ideas of Thaler and Sunstein, has been called Libertarian Paternalism. In their view, nudging is a technique of governments that aims to help people act rationally based on their own "true" interests. The government, as a choice architect, may exploit the cognitive biases and move *humans* toward rational choices. Sunstein (2016) postulates that nudging is ethically founded in social welfare, the autonomy of persons, and democratic self-government. To him, there is no alternative to nudging.

In the light of behavioural economics, a nudge is a function of any attempt at influencing people's judgment, choice, or behaviour in a predictable way. Nudging relies on cognitive boundaries and biases in individual decision-making that prevent people from performing rationally in their own self-interests. In this setting, the choice architecture encourages "better" decisions through behavioural interventions. It is supposed that authorities who know what is best for those individuals may change behaviours with the help of nudges. Different types of behavioural interventions by the government may help individuals make "better" decisions related to health, credit cards, consumer goods, or retirement plans.

The ideas of behavioural economics have been adopted by many governments and they have established specialized administrative nudge units to promote the use of these techniques. The former prime minister of the United Kingdom, David Cameron set up the Behavioural Insights Team (BIT), a special unit to develop behavioural policies, and invited Thaler as an informal advisor.[3] Barack Obama's most trusted advisors considered the behavioural economics research to promote social transformations.[4] Also in South Africa, this new approach has been used to fight severe water shortages, encourage smoking cessation, decrease drug and alcohol abuse, and reduce HIV transmission rates.

The target of Libertarian Paternalism is to maximize the expected subjective utility of individuals, while leaving those people who wish to ignore the default-rule free to opt-out at little cost. Indeed, they emphasize the cost of exercising choices and the preservation of freedom.

As people exhibit *extremeness aversion* – a tendency to avoid positions that are presented as extremes – Libertarian Paternalism has been presented as a middle-ground position between laissez-faire and Paternalism. Therefore, the debate relates not *whether* there should be paternalism, but *how much*. Indeed, the policy agenda of nudges exists on a *continuum* – defined by Thaler and Sunstein in a way that elides crucial distinctions between private and public, and between voluntary and coercive.

As a guiding principle for governance, Paternalism is nothing new (Kreider 2014). Paternalism is the policy of restricting the freedom and responsibilities of people in their own supposed best interest, like parents do with children. Libertarians directly oppose Paternalism, emphasizing that individuals know their own best interests better than any government possibly could, and that paternalism unjustly infringes on their liberty. Thaler and Sunstein have suggested that these two frameworks can be reconciled, and the resulting theory is coined Libertarian Paternalism or "new paternalism". This theory suggests that governments can set up rules to "nudge" citizens for their own good without restricting their freedom to make choices. Therefore, Libertarian Paternalism seeks to help citizens lead better lives by setting up rules that encourage a specific behaviour while allowing citizens to "opt-out" of the default.

To understand the relevance of Libertarian Paternalism in political philosophical thinking, the concept deserves attention from a historical perspective. Paternalism is opposed by the liberal tradition and is a recurring theme in political theory and ethics.

The challenge of freedom

Hayek and the rebirth of classical liberalism

As Chandran Kukathas recalls, the Austrian economist Friedrich August von Hayek started his intellectual life as an economist but turned his attention to political philosophy late in his career (Kukathas 2012). Through his life, his thoughts developed in a more libertarian direction. Indeed, he defended a philosophy of liberalism as an antidote to the development of totalitarian regimes. He became more sceptical about the role of the government in the provision of public goods because the political process was infected by particular interests.

According to Hayek, Adam Smith, and other philosophers of the Scottish Enlightenment, the founders of classical liberalism never viewed human behaviour as optimizing. Moreover, the Smithian tradition argues that in contemporary, complex societies, the main cognitive load in coordinating economic activity is borne by institutions rather than individual minds (Hayek 1948).

The contribution by Hayek stimulates a far-reaching debate on the role of the government in the markets and the effects of alternative policies. Indeed, the fundamental problem in economics, for Hayek, is that of coordinating the plans of many independent individuals. The main advantage of a competitive economic order, in Hayek's view, is that rational agents respond to price signals, which convey the relevant information available in the markets, for the purpose of economic calculus. In his view, competition, through the price market system leads to such coordination. The underlying criticism relies on arbitrary interventions related to the presence of the state in economic systems (Hayek 1944). After the Second World War, Hayek discussed the redefinition of the legitimacy of the state and stressed the need to defeat the growing state intrusion in a democratic framework. He privileged the analysis of the values that shape the interrelations of individuals in a free society. Assessing the practical superiority of the free-market dynamics over governments' actions, Hayek believed that no government can know enough to effectively plan the future path of the economy and society.

Further, central banks do not have the relevant information to correctly manage the money supply.

Hayek, in fact, restated the relevance of concepts and ideas proposed by the classical liberal philosophy so as to rebuild the foundations of constitutional governments to face the institutional decay in contemporary societies. In the 1970s, Hayek proposed the abolition of the government's monopoly over the issue of fiat money to prevent price instability (Hayek 1976). His defence of a complete privatization of money supply stemmed from his disappointment with central banks' management, which, in his opinion, had been highly influenced by politics. He warned that political interference over monetary policy and price stability is incompatible with social cohesion. At that time, Hayek's proposal of institutional reform relied on a denationalization of money in the framework of a free market monetary regime where only those currencies that have a stable purchasing power would survive.

The starting point of his economic analysis is the individual that is "inescapably ignorant" and whose limited reasoning is unable to totally unveil the complexity of the world. As individuals have an incomplete and fragmented knowledge of the world, the complex phenomenon of the market will never be fully known by them. However, these ignorant individuals are aware of their limitations and, through a process of experimentation, examine the facts and select the rules of behaviour that offer solutions to recurring problems (Hayek 1973). The selected rules of behaviour are products of the experience of generations and they should respect the principle of increasing opportunity for all. In fact, Hayek rejects the neoclassical conceptualization of the *homo economicus* and its full rationality, and paid attention both to change and trends. Instead of an equilibrium approach to the markets, Hayek adopted an evolutionary perspective where economic and social phenomena cannot be studied by methods of knowledge like mathematics.[5]

In the economic order, the role of the government is to ensure the existence of a free society (Hayek 1973). The principle of competition is, *par excellence*, the one that guides the creation of wealth and preserves individual freedom. And cultural evolution is a process of social learning where the products of civilization are the outcomes of unintentional trials and errors. Then, the survival of a complex society depends on the selection of rules that preserves competitive markets where people make choices. In this setting, the fundamental economic problem is that of the coordination of plans of many independent individuals. Without private property incentives, the coordination of plans might not take place.[6]

In truth, Hayek highlighted the importance of retaining the idea of citizenship at the centre of modern political debates and insisted that the welfare state policies were, *per se*, enemies of the classical liberal notion of freedom. Under his view, a capitalist market system of social exchange is primarily justified because it protects individual freedom, that is to say, freedom to the life of every human being *as an individual.* This system achieves the complex task of production and distribution through a process of voluntary exchanges where coordination is effectively achieved without coercion. The market, as the economic foundation of capitalism, is recognized as the basis of equality among people. His criticism reaches the so called "rational" interventions of the government, who aim to correct the market failures. Since this aim turns out to be contradictory, every intervention of the government, despite the targets, produces injustices and inefficiencies in the context of the order of the market.

Hayek rejected arbitrary interventions of governments in the economic order (Hayek 1944). After the Second World War, he discussed the redefinition of the legitimacy of the government and stressed the need to defeat the growing government intrusion in a democratic context. His point of departure was the institutional decay in modern capitalist societies and the need to rebuild the foundations of economic and political freedom by means of the strengthening of constitutional governments. Taking into account the connection between economic and political freedom, the Austrian economist discussed the challenges to social, economic and political development in a constitutional order. On behalf of the superiority of the economic outcomes of the free competitive order over the arbitrary interventions of the government, Hayek pointed out the need to restrain the power of the governments in the international settlement.

Hayek increasingly focused on the abuse of power. He suggested the abolition of the government's monopoly of issuing fiat money and making any money "legal tender" for all existing debts to preserve price stability. Hayek advocated the complete privatisation of money supply, as revealed by the views expressed in *The Constitution of Liberty*, in 1960, and those views presented in *Denationalisation of Money*, as of 1976. He clearly expressed his discontent with the history of the government management of money – mainly because of the orientation of Keynesian ministers of finance.

In particular, Hayek (1976, 118) noted that the popularity of "Keynesian" economics was due to the fact that:

> ministers of finance were told by economists that running a deficit was a meritorious act, and even that, so long as there were unemployed resources, extra government expenditure cost the people nothing, any effective bar to a rapid increase in government expenditure was destroyed.

The Austrian economist strongly emphasized the conflict between the two goals of economic policy: public interventions through spending finance and the regulation of a stable currency. For him, it is highly undesirable in any circumstances that funds for government spending should be provided by the creation of additional money. And Hayek (1976, 117) emphatically warned:

> If we are to preserve a functioning market economy (and with it individual freedom), nothing can be more urgent than that we dissolve the unholy marriage between monetary and fiscal policy, long clandestine but formally consecrated with the victory of "Keynesian" economics.

In other words, to preserve a market economy, central banks should not accommodate the financial "needs" of governments by keeping interest rates low and stimulating an inflationist bias. In his view, the Keynesian expansionary monetary policies destroy the equilibrating operation of the price mechanism and provoke major business fluctuations in a context of "unlimited democracy" where governments have power to confer special material benefits to particular groups.

Hayek condemned the growing participation of governments in the economic activities and the menace of their arbitrary interventions after the Second World War. Hayek's main concern was to show that the reconciliation of individuality and community depends on individual freedom. Indeed, he privileged the analysis of the values that shape the interrelations between individuals in a free society. In this attempt, the concept of common good is a social construction based on values, such as the inviolability of the person, individual freedom, and justice. In other words, the economic order is considered to be the best form of organization for contemporary societies and the legitimacy of the government should be based on its limited power.

The principles of Libertarian Paternalism

Thaler explains the origins of the expression Libertarian Paternalism. When he was presenting a paper at the University of Chicago on the "Save More Tomorrow" programme, a discussant from the Economics Department accused him of being a paternalist. After receiving the biggest insult that someone can be accused of at the University of Chicago, he answered, "Well, I guess, but there's no coercion here, so, maybe you should call me a libertarian paternalist" (Thaler and Sunstein 2008). That was the starting point.

Thaler and Sunstein's contribution to Libertarian Paternalism is just one part of a broader movement known as new paternalism. In the 2008 book titled *Nudge*, Thaler and Sunstein laid out their theory of Libertarian Paternalism, although they had been developing this concept for some time.[7] Libertarian Paternalism is somewhere in between a laissez-faire system and the traditional ("hard") paternalism. As Sunstein and Thaler (2003, 1162) state, it is a "comparatively weak and non-intrusive type of paternalism".

Libertarian Paternalism is the normative standard underlying behavioural political recommendations. In social philosophy, paternalism involves acts of coercion (restricting freedom of choice) aimed at improving the welfare of targeted individuals. It was assumed, explicitly or not, that a paternalistic state knows better than individuals themselves do what their true welfare is. Behavioural economics allows government intervention because of "behavioural market failures". Libertarian Paternalism aims at increasing the level of subjective welfare, something people cannot do by themselves due to cognitive limitations.[8] While the "old" paternalism tried to improve the welfare of individuals by taking away their freedom of choice, Libertarian Paternalism maximally preserves the freedom of choice while the government state should only structure the field of choice, leaving final decisions to individuals (Thaler and Sunstein 2003). Thaler and Sunstein believe that Libertarian Paternalism does not involve coercion.

They originally introduced the concept of Libertarian Paternalism in their 2003 essay of the same name published in the *American Economic Review* (Thaler and Sunstein 2003, 175). Here the definition of a "paternalistic" policy appears as "if it is selected with the goal of influencing the choices of affected parties in a way that will make those parties better off"; where policies may be selected with the goal of influencing the choices of affected parties in a way that will make those parties better off, but where there is no coercion involved. In the 2003 paper, they added that people are better off, as judged by themselves, rather than interpreting "better off" as earlier to be "measured as objectively as possible". According to Thaler and Sunstein (2008, 6), Libertarian Paternalism is a kind of "soft paternalism" because "private and public choice architects are not merely trying to track or to implement people's anticipated choices. Rather, they are self-consciously attempting to move people in directions that will make their lives better".

In their best-selling book *Nudge*, the notion of Libertarian Paternalism is further defined. It is described as a "movement" or "strategy" where people are free to do what they like and to opt out of undesirable arrangements if they want to do so Thaler and Sunstein (2008, 5).

At the beginning of *Nudge*, they give an example that refers to the "dilemma" facing the manager of a cafeteria since he realized that he can affect consumer decision-making based on the layout of the dishes.[9] Using this information, among several strategies, the manager could try to improve the clients' well-being, to arrange food randomly, to arrange food to reflect clients' own preferences, to prioritize favoured suppliers' offerings, or even to maximize profits. By arranging the food in order to put fruit before cakes on the counter, the manager can be considered a choice architect who frames the clients' decisions. Therefore, the manager turns out to nudge clients to choose those dishes that are the healthiest option. Indeed, as Thaler and Sunstein (2003, 1182) note, there is no way to avoid effects on behaviour and choices: "The task for the committed libertarian is not to avoid such effects but to preserve freedom of choice."

The Libertarian Paternalist conclusion is that the manager should seek to improve the students' well-being by making the consumer go out of the way for the junk food, but placing the fruit next to the check-out. The consumers will then buy more fruit and less junk food. The Libertarian Paternalists assert that this makes the individual better off in accordance to the individual's own judgment.

This principle is then applied to many areas of the law, including saving, investing, lending, social security, health care, and education, among others. Thaler and Sunstein also propose several specific areas to target, including financial decisions, health and education. In the financial realm, nudges encourage personal saving, smarter investing, and borrowing decisions. Health nudges influence new habits of eating, and school choices are the targets of educational nudges.

As Thaler and Sunstein highlight (2008, 10), Libertarian Paternalism fully respects the preferences of rational consumers and help people make decisions that will lead to better satisfaction of preferences according to their own judgements. These arguments lead Sunstein and Thaler to the conclusion that a transition is needed from the old, dogmatic, and anti-paternalist attitude that economic theory has traditionally followed, to a new, anti-dogmatic, and paternalist one (Sunstein and Thaler 2003, 1161–1162).

What are the guidelines for the practical implementation of the Libertarian Paternalist ideas? First, it is necessary to determine which preferences should be considered reflecting the "true" preferences of an individual. Individuals act against their own interests when making decisions "that they would change if they had complete information, unlimited cognitive abilities and no lack of self-control" (Sunstein and Thaler 2003, 1162). Those preferences that deviate from the ideal of rationality should be corrected by the state's paternalistic interventions. Second, it is necessary to determine the methods for the choice architect to nudge citizens, allowing for a variety of rules of thumb and principles to choose from. Through changing the framing of the policy, governments should account for cognitive biases to encourage people to act in their own best interest.

Sunstein's (2014) analysis about "the Paternalist's toolbox" provides details on the nature of regulation – i.e., what types of nudges governments are likely to use, and the impact they are designed to have. Sunstein also outlines four classes of nudges:

1) those that affect outcomes without influencing beliefs and actions (e.g., automatic enrolment);
2) those that influence actions without influencing beliefs (a civil fine);
3) those that influence beliefs as a route to influencing actions (educational campaigns); and
4) those that influence preferences as a way to influence actions, bypassing beliefs (graphic images on cigarette packets).

Thaler and Sunstein believe that people do not always want to face making active choices, and people shouldn't have to make choices over so many matters in which they could defer to experts, assuming of course that people can trust them.[10] Sunstein (2015, 18) presents four conditions under which a policy maker would be advised to implement defaults:

1) when the context is confusing;
2) when people prefer not to choose;
3) when learning is not important; and
4) when the population is homogenous along a relevant dimension.

The whole point of defaults is that people do not choose and need not even be aware that there is (or was) a choice to make. Defaults by definition aren't symmetric with respect to the alternative options, and the preferences of the individual are presumed, along with their consent.

Sunstein and Thaler (2003, 1162–1163) rejected the sceptical, "dogmatic anti-paternalism" of libertarians. In their view, this anti-paternalist dogma rests on the false assumption that people make decisions in their own best interest. Moreover, the anti-paternalists' misconception is that paternalism always involves coercion. According to them, in the Libertarian Paternalist approach, the opt-out method from the government preserves individuals' freedom and is not coercive because the less optimal choice is still allowed to be made. Indeed, Libertarian

Paternalism operates along a *continuum*. The *Libertarian* Paternalist would implement relatively costless opt-outs, while the Libertarian *Paternalist* who is "especially confident of his welfare judgments" would offer an opt-out, but at a real cost (Sunstein and Thaler 2003, 1185–1186).

In Sunstein's 2013 book *Simpler: The Future of Governments*, we can find more detailed answers. He advocates that simplifying regulation can be a better guideline for governments as this trend can save money and improve health. One year later, in the book, *Why Nudge? The Politics of Libertarian Paternalism*, Sunstein explicitly asserts the link between guided choices and the differences in the personal costs – understood as physical, psychological, and financial harms – that they generate. The relative weight of these costs should be assessed by reference to a graded notion of paternalism (Sunstein 2014, 51). This is where we see a dedicated discussion on ethics. He goes into great detail on Mill's harm principle as a talking point around different types of nudges, and their corresponding association with different shades of paternalism. That is, the harder the form of paternalism, the greater the costs to the individual in choosing the non-nudged option that is judged by the state/science as leading to harm (e.g., banning smoking in public places). Sunstein's (2014, 19) distinction between hard and soft paternalism is explored again in more detail in his 2016 book *The Ethics of Influence*.

The nudged "better" option is generally justified on ethical grounds because it serves the good of the individual and of society. Against the scepticism from the academic community on the ethics of nudging, Sunstein (2015, 157–173) suggests that a one-size-fits-all strategy may not be the most effective approach to behavioural change, although he is critical of personalizing nudges and considers these to be a problematic solution. He believes that people show a strong preference for nudges that are deemed to be transparent (e.g., educational campaigns that inform people of details that help them make better decisions), as compared to nudges that are opaque and operate in ways that are not obvious to anyone engaged in the choice environment (e.g., placing the food in a canteen so that the healthier options are presented first).

In his book titled *The Ethics of Influence: Government in the Age of Behavioral Science*, Sunstein (2016, 3) asks: "What are the ethical constraints on influence, when it comes from government?" His short answer is: welfare, autonomy, dignity, and self-government. He develops a defence of nudges on ethical grounds, mainly focused on the freedom to choose.

Information and incentives

Free to choose

The "heuristics of nudging" refers to any factor that significantly changes the behaviour of *humans*. This behavioural intervention relies on the fact that people display *small-change tolerance*, that is, a willingness to tolerate changes perceived as relatively small deviations from the *status quo*. Within this context, different kinds of nudges may be considered "soft" policy interventions based on Libertarian Paternalism:

- the provision of information toward rational persuasion;
- the provision of incentives;
- the addition and the removal of choice options.

Sunstein's defence of nudges focused on the freedom to choose certainly recalls the title of the book *Free to Choose*, written by Milton and Rose Friedman (1979) where the relevant question is: what is the proper role for governments?

Leaning on the classical liberalism of Smith, Friedman highlights four duties of the government:

- The protection of individuals from coercion from within the country and from without.
- The protection of individuals from the administration of justice.
- The preservation and strengthen of a free society.
- The protection of members of the community who cannot be considered responsible for themselves (madmen and children).

If limited carefully, governments can serve their societies while relying on voluntary cooperation and economic freedom. Friedman declared that economic freedom – the freedom to dispose of income as individuals wish in accordance with their own values – has been gradually eroded in the United States.

The book *Free to Choose* (1979) is centreed on the debate about the relations between the state and the markets. In the context of the post-war expansion of the welfare state, Friedman argued that markets are self-regulating. Starting from the premise of classical liberalism, Friedman maintained that there was an opposition between individual freedom and the economic structures that had characterized the post-war period. In the context of the economic crisis of the industrialized economies in the 1970s, his criticisms of state interventionism called for a rethinking of the economic policy framework. The policy instruments used to stabilize aggregate demand and stimulate economic growth were called into question by Friedman's restatement of the argument that self-regulated markets could guarantee rational choice, equilibrium, and freedom (Madi and Gonçalves 2010). Friedman defended the price mechanism as a social organizer. In his view, making markets more flexible by eliminating restrictions at both the international and the microeconomic levels would guarantee macroeconomic stability.

Friedman criticized the amount of personal and corporate taxes in America since the government turned out to be the major source of economic instability. As inflation is caused by a more rapid increase in the amount of monetary supply and today's government determines the quantity of money, the only cure for inflation is a lower rate of monetary growth. Moreover, a large bureaucracy and a flawed social security system are included among the institutional failures that prevent welfare since the outcomes of those institutions threaten economic freedom. As the institutional setup cannot be abolished overnight, he proposed a reform of the welfare system by replacing the various specific programmes with one method of income supplement – a negative income tax. His proposal would allow people to receive a fraction of unused allowances from the government, up to a specified maximum. Such a programme would assure every family a minimum amount in order to target poverty directly and to provide incentive to get a job. The reform of the welfare system would give individuals the freedom to provide for their retirements as they wish.

Taking into account the role of government in education, Friedman stated that government intervention led not only to enormous waste of taxpayer resources but also to a poorer school system where test scores declined, and violence and racial tensions arose. Against the centralized bureaucracy's decisions, Friedman proposed a voucher system that would provide parents greater freedom to make choices about their children's school and promote true equality of educational opportunity. In his proposal, a new financing system for higher education would end the imposition of taxes on the poor to subsidize the education of the rich.

Although Friedman was aware that his proposals were not politically feasible in 1978, he believed that at the end of the 1970s there was a turning of public opinion against big government and its waste, against taxes, and welfare programmes. This turning tide would bring back the old ideals of personal freedom and limited government that held sway in the nineteenth century. Friedman defended capitalism as a system that can improve the condition of the poor. However, when the market is controlled, the gap between the rich and poor only grows wider. Restrictions on economic freedom have a way of spilling over to affect other freedoms, like the freedom of speech and of the press. These examples, Friedman believes, demonstrate the interdependence of one freedom on others; "freedom is one whole, that anything that reduces freedom in one part of our lives is likely to affect freedom in other parts" (Friedman and Friedman 1979, 69).

In conclusion, Friedman reclaimed the lost freedoms. He asserts that a society that pursues freedom will have greater equality as a by-product, though it is not an accident. The free market enhances the opportunities of human beings to achieve their aspirations and to fulfil their potential. As Friedman says, freedom "preserves the opportunity for today's disadvantaged to become tomorrow's privileged and, in the process, enables almost everyone, from top to bottom, to enjoy a fuller and richer life" (Friedman and Friedman 1979, 149).

Free individuals can live in accordance to their own values and benefit other individuals as they follow their own pursuits. Recalling Smith's ideas, Friedman highlights that individuals should be *free to choose*.

Default rules

Borrowing the expression from Friedman without its context, Thaler and Sunstein say that Libertarian Paternalists state that people should be "free to choose". In particular, by adding paternalism to libertarianism, they aim to reinforce that freedom is preserved. The Libertarian Paternalist relies on the claim that choice architects set "default" rules to induce people, without coercion, to act in ways that better advance their own welfare – leading to longer, healthier, and better lives. As people can reverse the default position if they prefer, their freedom of choice is thereby preserved. Libertarian Paternalism tries to preserve freedom of contract by avoiding mandatory rules and relying instead on a framework of default rules and opt-out strategies.

As human decision-making and behaviour are influenced by cognitive boundaries and biases, the concept of nudge captures the fact that human behaviour can be changed in order to achieve particular aims while maintaining the freedom to make choices. Therefore, the concept of nudge refers to a non-coercive recommendation that could generate new habits of behaviour and actions. In the book *Misbehaving* (2015), Thaler showed how the concept of Libertarian Paternalism has been associated since the early 2000s with the idea that people need help to make rational decisions, although this kind of help cannot add restrictions to their choices. Year later, the use of "nudge" in discussions of public policy was proposed by Thaler and Sunstein in the 2008 book *Nudge*, and since then the normative activity generated by behavioural economics has been expanding in academic literature.[11] In *Fear of Falling*, Thaler (2010) addresses that the rationality of nudging is to set up default rules that help individuals achieve their true goals and improve their lives. The target of Libertarian Paternalism is precisely to devise policies that help but don't intrude.

Among the well-known examples of nudging, Sunstein and Thaler (2003) make recommendations concerning the choice of default options in retirement savings plan. As Libertarian Paternalists state, automatic enlisting should be the default option offered to employees because it would help ruling out errors associated with the lack of willpower or hyperbolic discounting. Taking into account employment contract options, the advocates of Libertarian Paternalism believe that in order to increase the employees' welfare, default rules should always be offered to them.

To sum up, nudging targets the "true" preferences and better choices. There is the assumption that policymakers are able to carefully evaluate the evidences, consider alternatives, consult unbiased experts, and act only when the benefits clearly outweigh the costs. The set of interventions include restrictions, taxes, and information disclosure schemes, among other tools used to design the "choice architecture", and to nudge boundedly rational individuals towards more reasonable behaviour:

- The establishment of restrictions associated with high-risk behaviours (e.g., banning smoking in public places, drug-use prohibition, or motorcycle helmet laws).
- The inclusion of deterring stories, threatening pictures and worrisome phrases on hazardous products (such as "Smoking kills" on tobacco).
- The application of "sin taxes" (high taxes) (e.g., on alcoholic beverages, tobacco, gambling, fatty products, and carbonated drinks).
- The addition of "cool-off" periods in the law before and after making decisions (related, for instance, to consumer legislation).
- The requirement of mandatory information disclosures in consumer credit transactions, mortgages, and loans.[12]

In other words, when addressing boundedly rational individuals in the context of Libertarian Paternalism, governments should rely not only on incentive schemes but also on preventive and restrictive measures (Saint-Paul 2011). The main idea is that governments should internalize externalities through public policy.

As the leader of the nudge unit in the UK states: nudging is about *conversion* not *compliance*. In his own words:

> For conversion, you need to persuade and convince, not force or insist. We have also to persuade ourselves that some neat ideas developed from lab experiments with North American students would really work in the real, nuts and bolts world of government policy and practice.
>
> (Halpern 2015, 274)

As Rizzo and Whitman (2009) warns, the *nudge continuum* tends to consider any form of government interventions as admissible if this intervention effectively influences human behaviour toward desirable (rational) ends. We can add that, in the context of Libertarian Paternalism, the use of reason in nudging people reveals the modern trend of rationalism in politics, as we shall discuss in the last chapter in this book.

Behavioural insights for policy change

The UK Nudge Unit narrative: what works?

Britain's Nudge Unit, BIT, was created in 2010, under the advisement of Sunstein. The social psychologist Robert Cialdini who had great influence on the treatment of marketing in business schools gave a seminar which influenced ministers towards nudging (1984/1993). In these pages, Halpern recalls the organization and outcomes of the seminar led by Cialdini (Halpern 2015, 34–36). Although Kahneman played a continuing role in forming the BIT's thinking, Thaler and Sunstein gave the principal stimulus for the creation of the BIT. Sunstein's example in government was essential for the establishment of the BIT and Thaler was similarly supportive, sitting on the BIT's Academic Advisory Panel.

The narrative of the Nudge Unit has already counted "successes", such as those related to a higher rate of tax compliance after nudging with the information "9 out of 10 of your neighbours are in compliance", and to an increase in overall energy efficiency after nudging people through incentives oriented to clear the attic of their homes and change energy practices.

Against the contemporary atmosphere of scepticism about politics, Halpern's book *Inside the Nudge Unit* (2015) celebrates behavioural interventions in the UK, claiming that the BIT's influence has already been remarkable. After the BIT improved health and transport conditions for people, higher revenues have been brought to the government (Halpern 2015, 350–351). Halpern is the principal founder and the continuing director and chief executive of the BIT. Halpern agrees that behavioural interventions are a better guide to governance in the twenty-first century. In the book, Halpern enthusiastically described the history and practices of the

British government. Although the point of departure of the nudge idea was under the prime ministership of Tony Blair, the creation of the BIT as a "unit" within the Prime Minister's Office was under David Cameron. The aim was to promote a major change in the methods of government policy and practice. In this attempt, the experimentation and the implementation of nudging have been based on mnemonics found in business literature, such as SNAP (Salience, Norms, Affect, Priming), MINDSPACE (Messenger, Incentives, Norms, Defaults, Salience, Priming, Affect, Commitments, Ego) and EAST (Easy, Attract, Social, Timely).

Following the "best" business practices, government experiments showed how nudging people could reduce carbon emissions, reduce smoking, help students finish their courses, and increase organ donation, among others examples (Halpern 2015, 9). After some years, the BIT's actual innovations involved a wide range of sectors:

- in the health sector, the introduction of new forms filled by the doctors reduced the number of errors,
- in the tax system, the redesign of the tax website improved the access to relevant information and increased the proportion of people completing their tax forms.
- in the labour market, the use of the nudge to reduce unemployment by changing the way Jobcentres work in order to provide a positive assessment to jobseekers (Halpern 2015, 120–122 and 197–205).

However, the most important changes in behavioural policies are around "method and mindset" in order to find out "what works" (Halpern 2015, 217). The focus on experimentation in policy design has fostered the expansion of "What Works Centres" in the UK – each of them is oriented to the local creation, transmission, and adoption of best practices. Centres for education and criminal reduction have been following the same methodology: gathering information and systematic trialling for collating evidences.

Although nudges should attract people for good, Halpern acknowledges that there is no neutral choice and pointed out some challenges in terms of transparency, efficiency, and accountability.

Nudges in public policy: the new frontiers

The application of behavioural interventions to date has largely focused on improving the implementation and delivery of alternatives to regulation, in particular through strengthening the information available to citizens and businesses to enable them to make better choices.

These behavioural insights (BI) have spread over 200 government units, initiatives, capacities, and partnerships established globally in every continent. The application has focused on improving implementation and the delivery of alternatives to regulation through strengthening the information available to citizens and businesses to make better choices.

The Organisation for Economic Co-operation and Development (OECD) report (2018) concludes that there is further potential in the use of behavioural economics in identifying the challenges that governments seek to address, such as: social inclusion and sustainability, both in developed and developing economies, as well as national, sub-national, and local government;. improving education and youth policies; creating safer communities; making more sustainable choices; and delivering better health services and outcomes. Following the seminal OECD Seminar on Behavioural Insights held in January 2015 and the OECD Nudging for Good Seminar held in May 2017, governments face challenges in how to implement behaviourally-informed policy interventions with responsibility.

Moreover, the 2017 Behavioural Insights Conference in Paris called for discussion on normative guidelines in order to carry out behaviour-oriented projects. This resulted from a perceived gap in the behavioural economics literature, whereby many prescriptive frameworks and case studies exist, but there are few resources oriented to help policymakers design, implement, and evaluate a BI project.

The OECD has been developing a project named BASIC that refers to a process-oriented framework that serves as a repository of best practices, proof of concepts and methodological standards for behavioural practitioners and policymakers. The BASIC project is built on five stages that guide the application of BI to any policy issue:

1. **Behaviour** deals with the initial stage of applying BI at the beginning of the policy cycle so as to target crucial behavioural problems versus systemic issues.
2. **Analysis** deals with the detailed examination of the target behaviours as viewed through the lens of BI.
3. **Strategies** provide guidelines for the practitioner to identify, conceptualise, and design behaviourally informed strategies based on behavioural analyses that result from Stages 1 and 2.
4. **Intervention** presents core methods for systematically designing and evaluating the efficacy and reception of behavioural interventions.
5. **Change** provides practitioners with tools for checking whether the initial assumptions and contextual factors have evolved before rolling out a BI-informed intervention and producing plans for

implementation, scale, monitoring, evaluation, maintenance, and dissemination of applications.

Within this methodology, the *how* is as important as the *what*. In other words, "what works" is defined after behavioural experiments, the aim of which is to gather relevant information to address local needs. Governments are encouraged to start by looking for "what works" in their communities in order to build narratives, establish collaborative frameworks, and adjust targets based on current resources and capacity. Therefore, experimentation in public policy is considered to be cost-effective and tailored to the local needs.

BI are currently being considered innovative solutions to face complex policy decisions. In order to achieve policy goals, the community is required to address four challenges:

1. Effective behaviour change requires consistent messages about what modifications are expected, and why they are relevant. For example, a government may promote sustainable transportation policies, but at the same time install a large number of new parking spots in city centres. These conflicting messages can lead to a loss of impact on behavioural changes.
2. BI depend on the responsibility of the behavioural community to be involved in the early stages of policy in order to help improve policy outcomes and identify current limitations.
3. BI in policymaking require investments in education and capacity building.
4. The behavioural communication strategies on what behavioural interventions are, what they can and cannot do, and how.

Effective organisational behaviour change is about getting the structure and proper incentives to overcome entrenched habits. Four options might amplify the use of BI:

1. Options need to be available and inclusive for marginalised populations.
2. Options need to be cost-effective as the lack of sufficient resources is a primary impediment in defeating social challenges.
3. Practitioners need to be aware of resource constraints as they advance behaviourally-oriented solutions.
4. Finally, the behavioural community needs to establish effective partnerships between government, academia, civil society organisations, business leaders, and different interested parties to improve innovative and implementable decisions.

Applying these guidelines to education requires changing attitudes, motivations, and creating a culture of respect, as these are noted as the main avenues for improving outcomes and re-engaging youth in education. In health care, behavioural policy recommendations requires the promotion of better choices and actions in early-stage screening of health care issues, such as diabetes, mental illness, and weight loss. Considering the public sector, the reduction of red tape and the improvement of recruitment practices are very important. In all the attempts, behavioural change initiatives should target political leadership, senior public servants, and officials who have different incentives for adopting or resisting reforms.

Governments should be supported to design and implement BI (OECD 2018). In this attempt, they should:

- Start building narratives that can be used to build a case for BI in government. Narratives are especially important for engaging and gaining support from leadership.
- Obtain political support so as to take advantage of a favourable climate. This may then start small behavioural interventions that can slowly gain support for the broader use of behavioural practices.
- Establish frameworks for collaboration with government and nongovernmental partners based on clear mandates and targets.
- Begin trial projects despite the lack of a large amount of resources.
- Combine experimentation and testing in order to build a methodology that best fits at the various stages of the policy cycle.

Conclusion

Behavioural policy interventions have become more widely applied in economic policy agendas. The target has been to improve the implementation of alternatives to conventional government interventions, in particular through strengthening the information and incentives available to citizens to make better choices. In the light of Thaler and Sunstein's contribution to behavioural economics, this chapter has highlighted the relation between nudges and Libertarian Paternalism. The conceptualization of Libertarian Paternalism deserved attention in historical and philosophical perspectives. In this attempt, Hayek's rebirth of classical liberalism and the Libertarian Paternalism of Thaler and Sunstein were analysed.

Libertarian Paternalists claim that the role of public policy is to improve the individual's decision making since humans are predictably irrational in various ways. Nudging tries to help people increase their level of subjective welfare, something they cannot do by themselves due to cognitive biases. Libertarian Paternalism maximally preserves the freedom of choice while government interventions frame choices, leaving the final decisions to individuals.

In 2011, the House of Lords Science and Technology Select Committee Inquiry on Behaviour Change reported that not enough was known about how governments can change or influence behaviour at a population level. The extensive report on behavioural change also highlighted that most of the available research is conducted exclusively on individuals, and it is simply inadequate to aggregate these findings up to social groups, communities, and whole nations. The main points reported were:

- Although nudging is useful for changing behaviours, particularly in the health sector, it is not a substitute for government regulation and it should be used within a framework of more traditional legislative and financial tools.
- Nudging has been promoted by the government as a soft, cheap alternative to more regulatory and infrastructural provisions.
- There is a lack of evidence on how effective social behaviour change can be achieved since it is not adequate to aggregate research findings from individuals without proper evidence of the real impacts on the population.
- Independent social scientists should advise government on the social effects of behavioural interventions not only to promote behaviour change across government but also to provide an evidence base of successful interventions.

The report goes much further in drawing attention to how governments should be working with businesses and voluntary organisations, and it also provides guidance on evaluating behavioural interventions. Moreover, it discusses the ethics of such programmes in relation to their intrusiveness and their transparency. In conclusion, the report puts in to question the definition of a "nudge" as well as the certainty of the "sciences of human behaviour". Indeed, it calls for a reflection on the methods and evidence of behavioural scientists.

Some years later, George Loewenstein, one of the founding fathers of behavioural economics, struck a note of caution on the euphoria surrounding the use of nudge-based solutions to addressing major public policy problems:

> Behavioral economics should complement, not substitute for, more substantive economic interventions. If traditional economics suggests that we should have a larger price difference between sugar-free and sugared drinks, behavioral economics could suggest whether consumers would respond better to a subsidy on unsweetened

> drinks or a tax on sugary drinks. But that's the most it can do. For all of its insights, behavioral economics alone is not a viable alternative to the kinds of far-reaching policies we need to tackle our nation's challenges.
>
> (Loewenstein and Ubel 2010)

It is time to consider the issue of how all these kinds of wisdoms reconfigure the human subject as an object of governance. The next chapter will provide a critical evaluation of the normative attitude of behavioural economics and its positive research programme. The chapter argues that the gradual transformation of a "welfare state" into a "paternalistic state" is one of the vital but poorly comprehended trends in the evolution of contemporary governance. Following the nudge proposals, the responsibility for public welfare has been shifted to individuals. While focusing on individual behaviours and choices, nudging people dismisses the global increasing economic, social, and political challenges at national, state, and local levels.

Notes

1 For a reflection on the changing relations between theory and aplied economics see Backhouse and Biddle (2000).
2 Weintraub (2002) discusses how economics became a mathematical science.
3 On this behavioural policy experience see Wintour (2013).
4 On the USA behavioural policy see Grunwald (2009).
5 Hayek believed that the Walrasian model was one of the best expressions of modernity, since it assumed, from the philosophical point of view, that the world could be unveiled by the power of reason and the use of a good method.
6 However, for Hayek, the problem of coordination is not associated with the problem of equilibrium. Equilibrium, by definition, is a state of affairs in which no agent within the system has any incentive to change because resources are used in the most efficient manner currently known.
7 See, for example, Jolls et al. (1998); Jolls and Sunstein (2006).
8 This aspect is discussed by Mitchell (2005, 1245).
9 See Thaler and Sunstein (2008, 1–6). This example also appears in Sunstein and Thaler (2003, 1164–1166).
10 See, for instance, Thaler and Sunstein (2008), Sunstein (2015), and Sunstein (2015).
11 On this point, read the analysis of Wright and Ginsburg (2012).
12 See the examples presented by Camerer et al. (2003).

References

Backhouse, R. and Biddle, J. (2000). The concept of applied economics: A history of ambiguity and multiple meanings. *History of Political Economy*, 32 (1): 1–24.

Camerer, C., Issacharoff, S., Loewenstein, G., O'Donoghue, T., and Rabin, M. (2003). Regulation for conservatives: Behavioral economics and the case for "asymmetric paternalism". *University of Pennsylvania Law Review*, 151 (1): 1211–1254.

Cialdini, R. B. (1984/1993). *Influence: The Psychology of Persuasion*, Revised edition. New York: W. Morrow.

Conference Report. Available at: www.oecd.org/gov/regulatory-policy/Behavioural-Insights-Conference-in-South-Africa-Summary-and-key-messages.pdf

Friedman, M. and Friedman, R. (1979). *Free to Choose: A Personal Statement*. New York: Harcourt Brace Jovanovich.

Grunwald, M. (2009). How Obama is using the science of change. *Time Magazine* April, p. 2.

Halpern, D. (2015). *Inside the Nudge Unit: How Small Changes Can Make a Big Difference*. London: WH Allen.

Hayek, F. A. (1944). *The Road to Serfdom*. Chicago: University of Chicago Press.

Hayek, F. A. (1948). *Individualism and Economic Order*. Chicago: Chicago University Press.

Hayek, F. A. (1960). *The Constitution of Liberty*. Chicago: University of Chicago Press.

Hayek, F. A. (1973). *Law, Legislation and Liberty*, Vol. 1. Chicago: University of Chicago Press.

Hayek, F. A. (1974). *The Pretence of Knowledge*. Nobel Prize Speech.

Hayek, F. A. (1976). *Denationalisation of Money: The Argument Refined*. London: Institute of Economic Affairs.

House of Lords. (2011). Science and technology select committee. *Behaviour Change*. Second Report of Session 2010–12. Published by the Authority of the House of Lords, 19 July 2011. London: The Stationery Office Limited.

Jolls, C. and Sunstein, C. (2006). Debiasing through law. *Journal of Legal Studies*, 35: 199–241.

Jolls, C., Sunstein, C., and Thaler, R. (1998). A behavioral approach to law and economics. *50 Stanford Law Rev.* 1471 (1998). Available at SSRN: https://ssrn.com/abstract=2292029.

Kapeliushnikov, R. (2015). Behavioral economics and the "new" paternalism. *Russian Journal of Economics*, 1 (1): 81–107, March.

Kreider, K. (2014). *New Paternalism. A Libertarian Treatment, but Not a Cure*. Economics Colloquium. Grove City College.

Kukathas, C. (2012). Friedrich Hayek and liberalism. In D. Edmonds and N. Warburton, *Philosophy Bites Back*. Oxford: Oxford University Press. pp. 230–249.

Loewenstein, G. and Ubel, P. (2010). The New York Times, July 14, www.nytimes.com/2010/07/15/opinion/15loewenstein.html (accessed January 20th, 2019).

Madi, M. A. C. and Gonçalves, J. R. B. (2010). Book review "Ideology and the international economy. The decline and fall of bretton woods". *Review of Political Economy*, 22 (2): 355–357.

Mitchell, G. (2005). Libertarian paternalism is an oxymoron. *Northwestern University Law Review*, 9 (3): 1245.

OECD. (2018). *Making a Real Difference: Nudging for Policy Change*. Paris: OECD Publishing.

Rizzo, M. J. and Whitman, D. G. (2009). The knowledge problem of the new paternalism. *Brigham Young University Law Review*, 4: 905–968.

Saint-Paul, J. (2011). *The Tyranny of Utility. Behavioral Social Science and the Role of Paternalism*. Princeton: Princeton University Press.

Sunstein, C. (2013). *Simpler: The Future of Government*. New York: Simon & Schuster.

Sunstein, C. (2014). *Why Nudge? The Politics of Libertarian Paternalism*. New Haven: Yale University Press.

Sunstein, C. (2015). *Choosing Not to Choose: Understanding the Value of Choice*. Oxford: Oxford University Press.

Sunstein, C. (2016). *The Ethics of Influence: Government in the Age of Behavioral Science*. Cambridge: Cambridge University Press.

Sunstein, C. and Thaler, R. (2003). Libertarian paternalism is not an oxymoron. *University of Chicago Law Review*, 70 (4): 1159–1202.

Thaler, R. (2010). Peace at last. *The Conversation*, 22 April. Avalilable at: www.cato-unbound.org/2010/04/22/richard-thaler/peace-last

Thaler, R. (2015). *Misbehaving: How Economics Became Behavioural*. London: Allen Lane.

Thaler, R. and Sunstein, C. (2003). Libertarian paternalism. *American Economic Review*, 93 (2): 175–179.

Thaler, R. and Sunstein, C. (2008). *Nudge: Improving Decisions about Health, Wealth, and Happiness*. New Haven: Yale University Press. p. 320.

Weintraub, E. R. (2002). *How Economics Became a Mathematical Science*. Durham: Duke University Press.

Wintour, P. (2013). "Nudge unit" to become profit-making. *The Guardian*. 1 May. Available at: www.theguardian.com/society/2013/may/01/policy-francismaude

Wright, J. D. and Ginsburg, D. H. (2012). Behavioral law and economics: Its origins, its fatal flaws, and its implications for liberty. *Northwestern University Law Review*, 106 (3): 1–56.

3 Behavioural economics

Methodological issues and philosophical concerns

Introduction

Behavioural economics developed a normative approach to government interventions (nudges) in order to help people change their behaviours and act rationally. This normative programme has been called Libertarian Paternalism by Thaler and Sunstein (2008). Indeed, behavioural economists have not abandoned the ideal of rationality in economics, since the intention–action gap toward rationality that motivates Libertarian Paternalist is ruled out *a priori*.

That is why Gilles Saint-Paul (2011) has stated that behavioural economics is the last bastion of rationalism in economic science and, in accordance with the same line of thought, Thomas C. Leonard (2008, 257) says:

> The irony is that behavioral economics, having attacked *Homo Economicus* as an empirically false description of human choice, now proposes, in the name of paternalism, to enshrine the very same fellow as the image of what people should want to be. Or, more precisely, what paternalists want people to be.

Through the transportation of the results of control trials to policy contexts, behavioural economics has spread a normative approach. As this chapter argues, the normativity of Libertarian Paternalism is built upon a methodology that can be analysed from a number of interrelated questions:

- How reliable are empirical data underlying the normative approach to behavioural policies?
- How convincing is the adoption of methodological individualism to justify government interventions?

Despite the non-uniformity of a population, that is to say, the existence of multiple anomalies, the normative recommendations are applicable by default to the entire society. This applicability is justified by the principles of Libertarian Paternalism where interventions impose almost no costs on rational individuals and preserve their freedom of choice.

In view of the methodological background of behavioural economics, a relevant topic for our analysis is whether economic policy-making should rely on the results of laboratory experiments and the interests are hidden behind.

The experimental setup

The transportation problem

Today, behavioural science, aims to identify patterns of individual behaviour. Its evidence-based scientific rigor is focused on causality: different behaviours are responses to identifiable stimulus and occur in a systematic pattern that supports predictions (Monsell 2017). In accordance with the situational determinism in behavioural economics, human behaviour is influenced by the framing of choices, that is to say, it is context-dependent (Mäki 2003, 17). Then, there is the belief that researchers can make predictions about human's conscious behaviour. As Liam Monsell (2017) argues, the dual challenge facing behavioural science is to formulate a theory that reflects real human behaviour in economic decision making, but also to acknowledge the limitation of the results of randomized control trials (RCTs) when extrapolating to other contexts.

Taking into account the relations between economics and psychology, Stefan Heidle (2014) states that psychology is treated as a mere add-on to mainstream economics and, therefore, behavioural economics faces the same methodological limitations. Looking back, theoretical and empirical work became more formal and mathematical mainly after the Second World War.[1] In this scenario, "measurement without theory", as Rutledge Vining (1949) explained, refers to empirical work as the main requirement to discover the appropriate theory.[2] The following debates were dominated by a methodological view, including Friedman's (1953) well-known contribution to the methodology in economics, which states that the only valid criticisms of a theory are the empirical ones. In Friedman's (1953, 14–15) own words:

> In so far as a theory can be said to have "assumptions" at all, and in so far as their "realism" can be judged independently of the validity of predictions, the relation between the significance of a theory and

> the "realism" of its assumptions is almost the opposite of that suggested by the view under criticism.... the relevant question to ask about the "assumptions" of a theory is not whether they are descriptively "realistic," for they never are, but whether they are sufficiently good approximations for the purpose in hand. And this question can be answered only be seeing whether the theory works, which means whether it yields sufficiently accurate predictions. The two supposedly independent tests thus reduce to one test.

By the 1970s, it was generally accepted that economics was based on a common core of economic theory cantered on mathematical modelling of maximizing agents. Moreover, the concern with applied economics became stronger among economists. Econometric models and formal statistical inference were widespread in applied research that not only has relied on computing capacity and new sources of data but also on arbitrary theoretical and statistical assumptions (Angrist and Pischke 2010). In the last decades of the twentieth century, the use of RCTs has also spread into economic research.[3] After the 1980s, the method of inquiry has been used in the evaluation of programmes in labour and welfare economics, among other fields.

Taking into consideration the development of behavioural economics from a methodological standpoint, its distinctive feature is the wide application of experimental methods.[4] Kahneman, similarly to other researchers in experimental economics, has developed methods for investigating economic behaviour in controlled laboratory experiments. Generally speaking, identifying errors and explaining them is the basic idea behind the heuristics and biases programme (Kahneman and Tversky 1974). The main goal has been "to understand the cognitive processes that produce both valid and invalid judgments" (Kahneman and Tversky 1996, 582).

The behavioural economics research programme is a clear departure from the "as if" methodology advocated by Friedman. The experiment-driven methodology of behavioural economics also supports that, in judging theories, the accuracy of the theoretical assumptions should be rejected as a good criterion and the accuracy of the theoretical predictions should remain as the most relevant criterion. The primacy of the accuracy of the theoretical predictions relies on the belief that replacing unrealistic assumptions with psychologically realistic ones should lead to better predictions. Therefore, the empirically-driven methodology of behavioural economics combines two practices:

- explicitly modelling limits on rationality, willpower, and self-interest; and
- using established facts to suggest assumptions about those limits.

Thaler believes that it is possible to make predictions about individuals or groups. And he added that the value of positive work lies in what the evidence shows. Regularities in human behaviour may be associated with general dispositions of various kinds – to avoid extremes, to comply with norms, to drink beer rather than wine – that manifest themselves in particular choices only in accordance with the context that frames the preferences. The understanding of different mental states and their relation to external forces may enhance a wide range of predictions about how different forces affect social behaviour. Therefore, the normative framework of behavioural economics can expand multiple possibilities for framing choices in public policy.

Currently, in behavioural economics, RCTs are seen as the most credible method of inquiry. The leader of the Nudge Unit in the UK, Halpern (2015, 277) proposed the concept of experimental government in order to highlight the relevance of a more experimental and empirical approach to public policy. Following experimentation as a routine policy and practice, the RCTs are at the core of finding out "what works best". While governments could gradually find out the interventions that really work, the results of trials that might be considered more or less effective could be managed by policy makers. The relevance of the experimental government can be noted in Halpern's words:

> Governments, public bodies and businesses regularly make changes to what they do. Sometimes these changes are very extensive, such as when welfare systems are reformed, school curricula are overhauled, or professional guidelines are changed. No doubt those behind the changes think they are for the best. But without systematic testing, this is often little more than an educated guest. To me, this preparedness to make a change affecting millions of people, without testing it is potentially far more unacceptable than the alternative of running trials that affect a small number of people before imposing the change to everyone.
>
> (Halpern 2015, 328)

From the methodological standpoint, behavioural economists search for empirical regularities in irrational behaviour is essentially inductive. In other words, as behavioural economics involves a high degree of context-specific randomness, the challenge of researchers has been to identify a huge variety of "anomalies" in human behaviours. In this attempt, one relevant topic is the "transportation" problem. Why can the results of RCTs be used in new contexts, such as in policy contexts?

Angus Deaton and Nancy Cartwright (2016) highlight that there are misunderstandings about what the RCTs can really accomplish. In any given RCT, the methodology of induction does not ensure that relevant causal factors are not neglected across the sample groups. Therefore, the results of the process of inference might be wrong. Indeed, the results of RCTs can be challenged *ex post*, after examining the composition of the control group and the factors considered in the experimental setting. Moreover, economists Steven D. Levitt and John A. List highlighted that human behaviour in RCTs can be affected by the selection of the individuals, the context, the evaluation of actions by others, and ethical issues (Levitt and List 2007, 154). Then, the findings in a laboratory setting may overestimate or underestimate the outcomes of real life interactions.

Deaton and Cartwright (2016) also reject the extrapolation of the results of RCTs in other contexts since the causality of the outcomes is context-dependent. Therefore, the decision-making in experimental settings depends on contextual factors that may be different elsewhere. Without an understanding of why the effects work on society, the laboratory results cannot be transported and the normative outcomes of economic research are put into question. In other words, if an intervention "works" within the control trial and makes people better off in the laboratory, there is no guarantee that this intervention actually does so in the real-world. RCTs, as an inductive method of inquiry, run the risk of considering *worthless casual relations* as *causalities* in the attempt of theorizing. "What works" in the laboratory does not necessarily works in real life.

By relying on an inductive method of inquiry, that can never be perfectly extrapolated across time and space to everybody, behavioural economics does not provide a reliable foundation for economic theory and policy (Angrist and Pischke 2010). Indeed, behavioural economics turns out to be a set of descriptions of certain behavioural reactions gathered in control trials without joining these under any particular synthetic theory (Wright and Ginsburg 2012; Heidle 2014). Further controversies have been focused on the institutional sterility of the laboratory environment.[5]

The tools developed by economists and the way they were applied to specific issues are largely shaped by how scientists and politicians envisioned the policy-making process, from policy-objectives to the design of solution and their evaluations (Backhouse and Cherrier 2014). The next chapter will analyse the "dark" side of nudging as small and subtle interventions that aim to influence and guide behaviours in the context of neoliberalism.

The knowledge problem

The knowledge problem in economic policy making is not new. Hayek, in his famous critique of central planning, hit upon it. From the libertarian standpoint, the knowledge problem constitutes an argument against Libertarian Paternalism. But in addition to the knowledge problem, there is also the slippery-slope risk.

In the 1940s, Hayek (1948) already emphasized the relevance of this problem because of the decentralized nature of information in the markets. The main advantage of the competitive economic order, in Hayek's view, is that rational agents rely on price signals which convey the relevant information available for the purpose of economic calculus. In his theoretical contribution to economics, he highlighted that only competition, through the price market system, leads to an efficient coordination of multiple decisions. Individuals act in their own self-interest and prices reflect the information available in society for the purpose of economic calculus. Indeed, prices are signals that support an extensive social division of labour in a context of individual freedom.

In this respect, he criticized the ideas of the so called "prophetic" economic discourses that believe in an eschatological end – such as the ideas of Marx (Hayek 1944). For the author, the economic path traced by an omnipotent reason was the best example of the road to serfdom. Hayek did not understand society as a rational machine that could be built by the deliberation of rational individuals.

For him, the relevant question is: how do economic agents learn in the market process? How do individuals get the required information to make possible the coordination of their plans with the plans of others in the markets? The market prices are signals that can be considered as the key institutional guides for human learning on behalf of the contextual nature of the discovery and use of knowledge. For him, market prices have an incentive role – as highlighted by the traditional neoclassical theory. Hayek claims that prices also play an informational role that has usually been neglected by those economists mainly concerned with equilibrium models.

According to Hayek, the growth of wealth is stimulated when governments do not interfere with individuals' freedom. In this respect, Hayek's critique of Keynesian economics relies on the arbitrary interventions of governments in the economic order. In the 1974 Nobel Prize speech, *The Pretence of Knowledge*, Hayek criticized the Keynesian recommendations to cure unemployment by creating patterns of resource employment that cannot be maintained without price instability and the disorganization of the economic activity. He condemned the use of anti-cyclical government spending to defeat unemployment and mitigate any slackening of economic activity. In his view, the maintenance of Keynesian policies produces inflation and leads to the disorganization of all economic activity. His attention was focused on the outcomes of monetary policies on relative prices, the misallocation of resources and, particularly, the misdirection of investments (Madi 2015).

Hayek emphatically condemned the Keynesian transformation of the discipline of economics and the promotion of social engineering. In his view, Keynesian macroeconomic modelling requires detailed knowledge about the current levels of consumption, investment, and public spending, besides the full-employment level of gross domestic product, and the precise effects of the multiplier on economic activity. In the case of such a complex phenomenon as the market, he believed that neither in macroeconomics nor in microeconomics can the economists gather all the required factual information to provide a full explanation of the economic phenomena. According to Hayek, Keynesian macroeconomics gives an unsatisfactory and sometimes misleading theoretical explanation of empirically observed causalities.

As of the 1970s, Hayek pointed out that political interference over monetary policy is incompatible with the preservation of economic freedom. After the Second World War, Hayek restated the relevance of concepts and ideas proposed by the classical liberal philosophy. His attempt was to rebuild the foundations of constitutional governments in order to face the institutional decay in contemporary societies. Assessing the practical superiority of the free market dynamics over governments' discretionary interventions, Hayek believed that no government can know enough to effectively plan the future path of the economy. In *The Constitution of Liberty* (1960), Hayek built his view on the limits of human cognition to highlight that no government can know enough about a society to plan its future effectively. Indeed, the government's true role is more modest: to create general and equally applied laws that constitute the matrix where the spontaneous interactions of individuals can occur in the economic order. In his view, economists do not have to play the role of political leaders or social engineers, but they should focus on the maintenance of price stability to preserve social cohesion.

From the Hayekian standpoint, the use of nudging might disorganize the economic coordination of multiple agents and render the whole process of spontaneous interactions of individuals less rational. In accordance with this perspective, the limited knowledge of individuals is not seen as an argument that justifies the expansion of the government interventions in the economy and, more broadly, in people's private life.

More recently, Rizzo and Whitman (2009) also recalled "the knowledge problem of paternalism". Indeed, to successfully implement behavioural policies, the choice architect must possess large amount of information. In particular, the state should know the following:

- the "true" preferences of individuals;
- which specific errors are made by individuals and in which specific situations;
- which biases prevent their achievement, the extent of those biases, and how they interact with other biases;
- what the cost of these errors is and the negative impact on welfare;
- whether individuals take any steps themselves to prevent their errors and, if they do, to what extent such steps are effective;
- how much people have already self-corrected their biases;
- how much self-correction will occur in response to policy; and
- how heterogeneous the public is on all of these dimensions.

Indeed, Rizzo and Whitman (2009) put in question whether the choice architect actually discovers everybody's subjective preferences and nudges them toward better decisions. The conceptualization of the choice architect turns out to favour the false notion that the central planner is capable of knowing people's preferences better than they themselves know them.

In real-world economies, the designers of nudges, or the choice architects, also suffer from cognitive biases.[6] However, the advocates of nudging would say that policy makers, as designers of the default rules, "do not need to *know*: they (and we) could test the variations and *find out what works best*" (Halpern 2015, 277). Indeed, behind nudging there is a particular conception of economic knowledge and economic policy making.

The ideal of rationality

The Cartesian narrative still captures attention

Behavioural economics is still located within the tradition of the representative agent of neoclassical theory. As Matthew Darling states:

> By calling the rational-actor model into question, behavioral economics threatened to pull the shaky edifice of economics down altogether … that didn't happen. … Ironically, the greatest contribution of behavioural economics may be something economics never

> managed to do on its own – mount a robust defense of the assumption of homogenous agents.
>
> (2019)

In accordance with this line of thought, Edward Fullbrook highlights in his recent book *Narrative Fixation in Economics* (2016, 45), the Cartesian view of human reality has deeply shaped the way neoclassical economics theorizes about the economic and social existence. Also behavioural economics is overwhelmed by the attempt to help people be rational (Harsanyi 1982, 55).

In Part II of the *Discourse of Method* (1973), Descartes presents four principles that should be followed in order to acquire knowledge:

1) Human beings cannot admit any ideas that are not absolutely clear.
2) Human beings must divide each problem in so many parts as appropriate for its best resolution.
3) Human beings should apply deductive reasoning to organize their thoughts from the simplest to the most complex ones.
4) The analytical-synthetic process of reasoning leads to true knowledge.

Descartes (1973) states that the first principle of his method focuses on the importance of doubt since we can never accept something as true without putting it into question. Applying geometry as a model of science, he considers it postulates not only universal and necessary but also clear and distinctive ideas. In his view, only clear and distinctive ideas are pillars of true knowledge.

Based on the second principle, Descartes builds his research method of analysis that isolates the clear and distinctive ideas from the most complex ones. His emphasis on the order of thoughts strengthens the role of mathematics in the method of pure inquiry. Moreover, the third principle of his method leads to a special kind of organization of thoughts that should start with the simplest ones and gradually rise to the knowledge of the more composed, while assuming an order between them (Descartes 1973).

Departing from the mathematical method of reasoning, Descartes arrives at the notion of order in scientific thought. In other words, once the human subject knows the simple elements of a problem, he can assume all the consequences that derive from those first ideas can be considered as absolutely certain. Those first ideas have the characteristics of clarity and distinction: they are known intuitively and constitute the pillars on which true knowledge relies.

Finally, Descartes reinforces the analytical-synthetic process of reasoning. Following the deductive method of pure inquiry, human knowledge grows throughout a rigorous chain of ideas. While the human subject applies deductive reasoning to create a chain of ideas, new thoughts link the simplest to the most complex ones. In this attempt, true knowledge can be obtained.

As a matter of fact, the Cartesian method aims at the discovery of truth and construction of true knowledge. Moreover, clarity, distinction, and order overwhelmed the *mathesis universalis* that is considered the pinnacle of the epistemic and ontological construction of Cartesian thinking. As Étienne Gilson (1945) highlighted, the Cartesian method represents an attempt to extend the *mathesis universalis* to all human knowledge.

The *mathesis universalis* turns out to be a general method of inquiry that explains everything regardless of the objects to be studied. Reason alone has the ability to know the truth without the intervention of feelings or emotions. This conceptualization of human beings is overwhelmed by a subjective idealism that dismisses the social and historical setting. As a result, the theoretical contributions of neoclassical economics and behavioural economics turn out to move human beings out of real life experiences.

Then, we can say that the *cogito* is at the centre of the conceptualization of the *homo economicus*. This assumption suggests replacing ordinary people with the fully rational human being.

Deconstructing the thinking human subject

In the context of the second half of the nineteenth century, Nietzsche (1844–1900) laid new foundations for the understanding of the behaviour of human beings. His contributions were developed in an historical context characterized by the advance of psychology as "science" and the elaboration of criticisms of positivism. Singularity or universality, life as action or reaction, and conscious or unconscious attitudes were among his concerns.

Nietzsche condemned the development of a philsophical stadpoint based on the notion of the eternal human "soul" (Nietzsche 2012a). He penetrated the deep nature of the problem of human rationality and promoted the deconstruction of the Cartesian rational man of modernity. Moreover, the philosopher called for a reflection about the concept of human rationality that underlies positivist psychology. Then, his philosophical reflection favours an understanding of human conflicts and contradictions.

First of all, the philosopher aims not only at deconstructing the metaphysical foundations of the Cartesian rational being, but also to criticize the use of the positivist method of inquiry in psychology. Nietzsche stated that this method – cantered on causes, effects, and regularities – is not adequate enough to develop knowledge about people's lives. He rejected the mechanistic view of psychology of his time and proposed an innovative psychology that calls for a reflection on the conscious and unconscious elements that regulate the psychic life. In this sense, his innovative psychology rejects the immediate observation of conscious acts – like instincts – since they are not observable in empirical research.

Nietzsche (2012b, 7) noted that there are blockages in the passage of unconscious representations and desires to consciousness. In fact, affections, feelings, and instincts raise relevant questions about the psychic life that anticipate Freud's elaborations in psychoanalysis (Gay 2012). In accordance with Freud's ideas (2006), man has no conscious knowledge of the totality of his feelings. In this way, psychoanalysis seeks to give meaning to what is unconscious in human behaviour.

The philosopher brings to light the obscure dimension of existence since there are unconscious resistances that reveal contradictory inner conflicts. Nietzsche called himself the first "psychologist" and his view of the philosopher-psychologist privileges an artistic sensibility that can help overcome the interdictions created by culture – mainly by religion and science (Marton 2000). Psychology as a scientific knowledge should investigate the emergence and development of moral feelings (Nietzsche 2012c, 43).

In the book *The Genealogy of Morals* (2012b), Nietzsche emphasized the genealogy of moral values. Valuation and the hierarchy of values change over time as they relate to historically constructed social and cultural institutions. Then, psychology and history are interconnected since the constitution of subjectivity occurs in historical contexts where different power mechanisms influence the emergence of values. His innovative psychology highlights the existence of multiple internal forces in human life, where outcomes are not deterministic.

In fact, Nietzche highlighted the modes of valuation at the heart of the human psychological domain (Nietzsche 2012b, 9). His understanding of Western societies highlights that resentment and guilt occupy a prominent role in the emergence of values that favour reactive attitudes which empty the force of life itself. In other words, different modes of valuation operate on the constitution of subjectivities that shape different attitudes. The originality of this conception refers to a critique of the positivist psychology of his time that privileged the concepts of human rationality and adaptation. In his view, human lives are not homogeneous since there are different modes of valuation that impact on the subjectivities and shape human singularities.

For Nietzsche (2012d, 29), the overcoming of the human inner conflicts requires self-understanding of the unconscious impulses and the acceptance of the tragic nature of life as it is. This is the first step to the re-creation of the human being in the world. Indeed, the inner forces of denial and affirmation become crucial to build the singularity of human identity.

In his analysis about human rationality, Nietzsche emphasized that human beings are under permanent construction in a historical process where their subjectivities reveal modes of valuation and hierarchy of values (Deleuze 1976). Thus, Nietzsche's thoughts open space for the diversity in human behaviour that should be analysed in a cultural and historical perspective.

After Nietzsche, Foucault also called for a reflection on the deconstruction of the conceptualization of the homogenous rational human being as an anthropological universal. In the book *The Order of Things*, Foucault refused to accept the *cogito* of the Cartesian philosophy – understood as the "being" whose nature is to think and is endowed with the autonomy of reason (1981, 445). Descartes founded modern philosophy on a metaphysics that presents the *cogito* as its first principle. The certainty of the "I think, therefore I am" refers to the identity of the rational subject. In *Discourse of Method*, the conceptualization of the human being refers to a dualistic conceptualization of substances. Although soul and body are conceived as distinct substances, the man is the result of a substantial union: on the one hand, an intangible, immaterial substance, and, on the other hand, a material substance that refers to the mechanical structure of the body. For Descartes, errors of thinking could be avoided by the use of reason (1973).

Foucault proposed a modern *cogito* in order to move away from Descartes, since "I think" does not lead to the evidence of "I am" (Foucault 1981). The identity of the modern *cogito* considers human experiences in historical time and has a normative dimension. In the book *Discipline and Punish* (1995), Foucault analysed the normative dimension of subjectivity. In this attempt, he highlighted that human beings are trapped within power discipline and practices of domination that affect their subjectivity. In this sense, subjectivity cannot be considered as the result of self-awareness, but it is an historical-discursive construction. There is no dualism between subject and object, characteristic of the Cartesian philosophy, but subject and object change incessantly in the context of the evolution of social relationships, practices, and institutions (Foucault 1981, 229) Through the analysis of the historical ways of thinking and acting, Foucault called for a reflection on the objectification of the subject and its relation with procedures and techniques of power in the contemporary institutional setup.

Power, in his perspective, is understood as a mechanism of normalization put into action by a set of social institutions. In modern Western societies, surveillance becomes an essential component of power practices disseminated in multiple institutional forms that are related to disciplinary devices and different modes of subjectivation.

Positive results and normative claims

Empirical anomalies as a focal point

Behavioural economists have criticized the axioms of rational choice theory when reporting empirical "anomalies". Indeed, the conceptualization of the anomaly is a focal point of behavioural economics and its understanding refers to the role of a set of cognitive biases. Therefore behavioural economics is often conceived as the study of anomalies superimposed on a rational system (Gigerenzer 1991).

Kahneman (2003a, 163) explains that the study of cognitive biases does not dismiss the rational human being as a standard of comparison. And he clearly states: "theories in behavioural economics have generally retained the basic architecture of the rational model, adding assumptions about cognitive limitations designed to account for specific anomalies" (Kahneman 2003b, 1469). The cognitive biases are defined as a systematic discrepancy between a person's judgment and a norm, that is to say, the norm of rational behaviour. Kahneman and Tversky (1982, 157) consider that the deviations of behaviour and judgments from the rational norm are justified by cognitive illusions. In their view, it is possible to define one kind of behaviour, the rational, as the correct one.

Their focus is on the identification of empirical anomalies, in other words: the deviations from the norm. In accordance with Smith (2005, 144), an empirical anomaly is the difference between the rational behaviour described by a model of national choice and actual observed behaviour.

Rethinking normalization

In the middle 1970s, Foucault argued, in his lectures at the Collège de France, that the creation of the new conjunction of (bio) power and knowledge is at the core of the conceptualizations of the nature and function of the norm and normalization in modernity. The philosopher saw the norm as being at the heart of these techniques of modern power. Different normal curves are produced by studying a population, from those normal curves the norm gets established as an optimal or ideal normal which is then brought back to bear on the population in order to regulate that population – that is, to dictate how the population ought to behave.

Looking back, Foucault described the genealogy of norms. In the nineteenth century, he highlighted the larger framework to the constitution of the notion of abnormal (criminal) that was closely related to those who violate both human and natural law. Then, the spread of population statistics enhanced further possibilities for individual inter-comparison. The outcomes of these measurements installed the conceptual basis for thinking new techniques of control and management over population by qualifying people with quantifiable qualities. The aim is to influence people toward the normality.

In the lectures at the Collège de France that were focused on the topic of abnormality, the philisopher stated that the exercise of certain power is founded and legitimized by certain norm(s) (Foucault, 2003). In a disciplinary context, the norm is attached to a principle of both qualification and correction, as Dianna Taylor clarifies (2009). Indeed, the norm provides the grounds for government intervention and for distinguishing "normal" and "abnormal" individuals and populations.

Foucault warned that the norm (the ideal or optimal model) has a prescriptive character in the sense that the it determines what is normal. Power techniques that presuppose the (rational) norm are associated with techniques of intervention and transformation that affect humans' subjectivity and behaviour. In summary, the norm establishes what is normal and the statistical analysis constitutes a key technique for regulating and managing populations toward the normal. On the one hand, individuals and populations are brought into conformity with some particular social norms. On the other hand, in doing so, such techniques perpetuate power relations of the socio-political landscape to the point that they come to be seen not as produced at all but simply as natural and necessary (Foucault 2007).

Such naturalization of behaviours effectively promotes acceptance and conformity with prevailing norms on both an individual and societal level.

Conclusion

The spread of nudges raise concerns about whether economic policy should be built upon observations in the setting of laboratory experiments. Behavioural economics has not abandoned the Cartesian narrative deconstructed by Nietzsche and Foucault, among others, in the last centuries. Relying on Foucault's analysis on normalization in modern societies, this chapter proposed a reflection on the normativity of behavioural economics.

In summary, nudges as social norms establish what is normal (rational). Therefore, individuals and populations are brought into conformity with these particular social norms. In doing so, such techniques of modern governmentality perpetuate the power relations of the socio-political landscape to the point that they come to be seen as natural and necessary.

Notes

1 See Renfro (2011) for an analysis of the relations between economics and computers.
2 Backhouse and Cherrier (2014) highlight that little work has been done to explain both unification and fragmentation in economics and how practices and cultures vary among different trends in applied economics.
3 On this development, see Wise and Hausman (1985), Manski and Garfinkel (1992) and Gueron and Rolston (2013).
4 According to Backhouse and Cherrier (2014), little work has been done to explain both unification and fragmentation and how practices and cultures vary among different trends in applied economics.
5 See, for example, Levitt and List (2007), Knetsch (1989), and Plott and Zeiler (2007, 2011).
6 See, for instance, Grüne-Yanoff and Hertwig (2016, 166–167) and Berggren (2012).

References

Angrist, J. and Pischke, J.-S. (2010). The credibility revolution in empirical economics: How better research design is taking the con out of econometrics. *Journal of Economic Perspectives*, 24 (2): 3–30.

Backhouse, R. and Cherrier, B. (2014). *Becoming Applied: The Transformation of Economics after 1970*. Department of Economics Discussion Paper 14-11. University of Birmingham. Available at: www.birmingham.ac.uk/Documents/college-social-sciences/business/economics/2014-discussion-papers/14-11.pdf

Berggren, N. (2012). Time for behavioral political economy? An analysis of articles in behavioral economics. *The Review of Austrian Economics*, 25 (3): 199–221.

Darling, M. (2019). *Neoliberalism after Behavioral Economics*. Behavioral Scientist Blog. Available at: https://behavioralscientist.org/neoliberalism-after-behavioral-economics/

Deaton, A. and Cartwright, N. (2016). Understanding and misunderstanding randomized controlled trials. *NBER Working Paper* No. 22595.

Deleuze, G. (1976). *Nietzche e a filosofia*. Rio de Janeiro: Ed. Rio.

Descartes, R. (1973). *Discurso do Método (Discourse of Method)*. J. Guinsburg and B. P. Júnior (Trans.). São Paulo: Abril Cultural.

Foucault, M. (1981). *As Palavras e as Coisas (The Order of Things)*. São Paulo: Martins Fontes.

Foucault, M. (1995). *Discipline and Punish: The Birth of the Prison*. New York: Vintage Books.
Foucault, M. (2003). *Abnormal: Lectures at the Collège De France 1974–1975*. V. Marchetti and A. Salomini (Eds.). G. Burchell (Trans.). London: Verso.
Foucault, M. (2007). *Security, Territory, Population: Lectures at the Collège de France 1977–1978*. Graham Burchell (Trans.). New York: Palgrave.
Freud, S. and Inconsciente, O. (2006). *Obras Psicológica se Sigmund Freud. Escritos sobre a Psicología do Inconsciente, 1915–1920*, Vol. II. Rio de Janeiro: Imago.
Friedman, M. (1953). The methodology of positive economics. In *Essays in Positive Economics*. Chicago: University of Chicago Press. pp. 3–43.
Fullbrook, E. (2016). *Narrative Fixation in Economics*. UK: WEA Books.
Gay, P. (2012). *Freud: uma vida para nosso tempo*. São Paulo: Companhia das Letras.
Gigerenzer, G. (1991). How to make cognitive illusions disappear: Beyond "heuristics and biases". *European Review of Social Psychology*, 2: 83–115.
Gilson, É. (1945). Introducción. In: Descartes, R. (Eds.), *Obras Filosóficas*. Buenos Aires: Editorial El Ateneo.
Grüne-Yanoff, T. and Hertwig, R. (2016). Nudge versus boost: How coherent are policy and theory? *Minds & Machines*, 26 (1): 149–183.
Gueron, J. M. and Rolston, H. (2013). *Fighting for Reliable Evidence*. New York: Russell Sage.
Halpern, D. (2015). *Inside the Nudge Unit: How Small Changes Can Make a Big Difference*. London: WH Allen.
Harsanyi, J. (1982). Morality and the theory of rational behaviour. In A. Sen and B. Williams (Eds.), *Utilitarianism and Beyond*. Cambridge: Cambridge University Press. pp. 39–62.
Hayek, F. A. (1944). *The Road to Serfdom*. Chicago: University of Chicago Press.
Hayek, F. A. (1948). *Individualism and Economic Order*. Chicago: Chicago University Press.
Hayek, F. A. (1960). *The Constitution of Liberty*. Chicago: University of Chicago Press.
Hayek, F. A. (1974). *The Pretence of Knowledge*. Nobel Prize Speech.
Heidle, S. (2014). *Philosophical Problems of Behavioural Economics*. PhD dissertation, University of Bonn.
Kahneman, D. (2003b). Maps of bounded rationality. *American Economic Review*, 93 (5): 1449–1475, December.
Kahneman, D. and Tversky, A. (1974). Judgment under uncertainty: Heuristics and biases. *Science*, 185 (4157): 1124–1131.
Kahneman, D. and Tversky, A. (1982). Variants of uncertainty. *Cognition*, 11 (2): 143–157.
Kahneman, D. and Tversky, A. (1996). On the reality of cognitive illusions. *Psychological Review*, 103 (3): 582–591.
Kahneman, D. (2003a). A psychological perspective on economics. *American Economic Review (Papers and Proceedings)*, 93 (2): 162–168, May.

Knetsch, J. L. (1989). The endowment effect and evidence of nonreversible indifference curves. *American Economic Review*, 79 (5): 1184–1277.

Leonard, T. C. (2008). Review of Richard H. Thaler, Cass R. Sunstein, nudge: Improving decisions about health, wealth, and happiness. *Constitutional Political Economy*, 19 (4): 356–360.

Levitt, S. D. and List, J. A. (2007). What do laboratory experiments measuring social preferences reveal about the real world? *Journal of Economic Perspectives*, 21 (2): 153–174.

Madi, M. A. C. (2015). Dissolving "the unholy marriage": Hayek's recommendation on monetary and fiscal policy. *Journal of Contemporary Economic and Business Issues*, 2 (2): 23–38.

Mäki, U. (2003). Economics with institutions: Agenda for methodological enquiry. In B. Gustafsson, C. Knudsen, and U. Mäki (Eds.), *Rationality, Institutions and Economic Methodology*. London: Routledge. pp. 3–42.

Manski, C. F. and Garfinkel, I. (1992). *Evaluating Welfare and Training Programs*. Cambridge, MA: Harvard University Press.

Marton, S. (2000). *Nietzsche: das forças cósmicas aos valores humanos*. Belo Horizonte: UFMG.

Monsell, L. (2017). The game of life: Discussing determinism in behavioural science. *The Decision Lab*, June.

Nietzsche, F. (2012a). *Além do Bem e do mal*. São Paulo: Companhia das Letras.

Nietzsche, F. (2012b). *Genealogia da Moral (The Genealogy of Morals)*. São Paulo: Companhia das Letras.

Nietzsche, F. (2012c). *Humano, Demasiando Humano (Human, All Too Human)*. São Paulo: Companhia das Letras.

Nietzsche, F. (2012d). *O Nascimento da Tragédia (The Birth of Tragedy)*. São Paulo: Companhia das Letras.

Plott, R. and Zeiler, K. (2007). Exchange asymmetries incorrectly interpreted as evidence of endowment effect theory and prospect theory? *American Economic Review*, 97 (4): 1449–1466.

Plott, R. and Zeiler, K. (2011). The willingness to pay-willingness to accept gap, the "endowment effect", subject misconceptions, and experimental procedures for eliciting valuations: Reply. *American Economic Review*, 101 (4): 1449–1466.

Renfro, J. A. (2011). Econometrics and the computer: Love or a marriage of convenience. *History of Political Economy*, 43 (Annual supplement): 86–105.

Rizzo, M. J. and Whitman, D. G. (2009). The knowledge problem of the new paternalism. *Brigham Young University Law Review*, 4: 905–968.

Saint-Paul, J. (2011). *The Tyranny of Utility. Behavioral Social Science and the Role of Paternalism*. Princeton: Princeton University Press.

Smith, V. L. (2005). Behavioral economics research and the foundations of economics. *Journal of Socio-Economics*, 34 (2): 135–150.

Taylor, D. (2009). Normativity and normalization. *Foucault Studies*, 7: 45–63, September.

Thaler, R. and Sunstein, C. (2008). *Nudge: Improving Decisions about Health, Wealth, and Happiness*. New Haven: Yale University Press.

Vining, R. (1949). Methodological issues in quantitative economics: Koopmans on the choice of variables to be studied and of methods of measurement. *The Review of Economic and Statistics*, 21 (2): 77–86.

Wise, D. A. and Hausman, J. A. (1985). *Social Experimentation*. Chicago, IL: Chicago University Press for NBER.

Wright, J. D. and Ginsburg, D. H. (2012). Behavioral law and economics: Its origins, its fatal flaws, and its implications for liberty. *Northwestern University Law Review*, 106 (3): 1–56.

4 Nudging citizens in the context of neoliberalism

Their hidden side

Introduction

The neoliberal agenda represents the intellectual victory of Hayek's ideas about the supremacy of the competitive economic order. Hayek highlighted that it is not capitalism that is responsible for the emergence of social problems, and criticizes the government interventionism to promote welfare. Against, the "welfare state", Thaler and Sunstein (2003) propose a "Libertarian Paternalistic state." In this context, nudges are becoming an increasing part of the daily lives of individuals, consumers, and citizens.

In this setting, much of the debate about nudging has emphasized this tool as a more efficient, effective, and ethically justifiable alternative to more coercive governmental strategies (Sunstein 2015). The applications of the nudge as a corrective for "behavioural market failures" turned out to be a new mode of "behavioural" governance under which the government manages and enacts policies that are intended to influence behaviours in order to help people make better life choices.

Considering everything, the relevant question is: what are the reasons that explain the increasing acceptance of the nudge approach to public policy?

First, the use of nudges in public policy has been designed in the context of financialization where global market deregulation affected the goals of governments and the evolution of businesses. Second, the focus on individual behaviour is consistent with a neoliberal agenda where the new perspectives on public policies enhance the *illusion of free individual choice.*

Third, behind the partnerships between the public and the private sectors that aim at developing new forms of non-coercive regulations, there is, in truth, a set of economic and political interrelations that shape the financialization of corporate strategies in sectors that used to be related to public services. In this context the government shifts the responsibility for health care, employment, education, and welfare to individuals (Ramsay 2012). And finally, it is worth noting that, while putting emphasis on individual behaviours and choices, the nudge approach to policy-making dismisses the global increasing economic, social, and political challenges at national, state, and local levels.[1]

This chapter addresses that behind nudging there are well-known mechanisms of neoliberal governance that promote rationalism in politics as well as an apolitical discourse on individual responsibility. Moreover, these mechanisms enhance the decentralization practices at the community level and the self-governance of individuals aligning their preferences in accordance to a market-based rationality.

Transformations in governmentality

The big picture

The dark side of nudges should be analysed taking into account the political, social, and economic challenges in a broader context and in a longer perspective. Since the 1970s, the advance of the process of economic deregulation has been supported by the legitimization of this discourse on neoliberalism. The political, economic, and social dimensions of the neoliberal transformations represent a rupture in relation to the relative order of the Cold War era (Leeson 2003).

From a national perspective, the redefinition and reorientation of the scope of the state's actions have re-shaped the global relations between nation-states and the increasingly transitional business sector. In the framework of economic integration, global investors punish those governments whose economic policy options do not favour market flexibility and financial stability. In this scenario, the challenges of growth and development at the beginning of this century are turning out to be more complex and reveal that the global challenges require supranational solutions to supranational or transnational problems. Currently, there is no global authority to assume these political decisions. Neither the World Bank, nor the International Monetary Fund, nor even the World Trade Organization is able to do this (Hobsbawm 2007).

In addition to these social and economic challenges, nations and nationalism have been affected by the collapse of the international balance of political power since the Second World War has fostered new trends in politics. Looking back to the twentieth century, the roots of this scenario can be related to the collapse of the post-war international balance of power. Today, the lack of a clear distinction between times of war and peace threatens individual freedom and engenders insecurity in social relations. In this setting, especially since September 11, the "war against terror" has justified powerful mechanisms of control on individuals. There seems to be a general crisis of state power and state legitimacy (Hobsbawm 2007, 51).

In the context of neoliberal governance, new forms of political power and cultural changes are related issues that shape current livelihoods. In fact, the material and non-material elements of a society should be considered in any attempt to apprehend the challenges to overcome the process of social change. Currently, we can note that the recent transformations in global capitalism have shown that the current capitalist institutional set-up is an embodiment of the "economic motive" as an expression of the global cultural practices spread in the context of financialization. The effects of the big financial business on the enlargement of the market exchange relations could be apprehended in the context of the unrestricted markets where one decisive driving-force of the global dynamics is related to the spread of the "culture of money". In this scenario, the political dominance of high finance comes about by shaping new elites and cultural practices. The free-market capitalist culture and its market institutions and values are dismantling the traditional ones, such as the value of generosity. This process enhances the loss of social ties since individual claims are threatening the preservation of social interests. On the whole, social inequality turns out to be an outstanding feature of current globalization.

Current concerns about social justice and peace in the global order demonstrate the relevance of the ideas of Eric Hobsbawm in his 2008 book *Globalisation, Democracy and Terrorism* where he explored the inner tensions that have shaped the de-regulated economies. Hobsbawm attempted a comprehensive reflection on the human condition at the beginning of the twenty-first century. In his view, people are living in a period of economic instability, social insecurity, and barbarization, while nation-states try to cope with issues of public order and changes in the international balance of power.

Indeed, there is world-wide evidence that indicates serious threats to social cohesion and justice in current capitalist societies. In light of those threats, Hobsbawm sharply noted that:

> They seem to reflect the profound social dislocations brought about at all levels of society by the most rapid and dramatic transformation in human life and society experienced within single lifetimes. They also seem to reflect both a crisis in traditional systems of authority, hegemony and legitimacy in the west and their breakdown in the east and the south, as well as a crisis

> in the traditional movements that claimed to provide an alternative to these.
>
> (Hobsbawm 2007, 137)

The extraordinary acceleration of globalization since the 1970s has been characterized by some relevant features. First, contemporary free-market globalization has ultimately led to an increase in economic and social inequalities not only within states, but also internationally, despite the presence of a decreasing trend in extreme poverty. Second, the self-regulated market has undermined the ability of nation states and welfare systems to protect those who rely on income from wages or salaries. Third, in view of the social impacts of globalization, recent evidence indicates threats to social cohesion and justice in current capitalist societies. Finally, the deep cultural impacts of globalization have been strengthened by the diffusion of new social norms that influence behaviours. In truth, the process of globalization turned out to require not only a set of recommendations for economic integration, but also the homogenization of attitudes and behaviours all round the world. Indeed, the access to international finance interacts with cultural features. In this scenario, the global governance rules have reorganized main features of economies and societies.

As Kari Polanyi-Levitt (2013) explains, since the early 1980s, many Western economies observed the declining contribution of manufacturing and the increasing contribution of finance, distribution and business services to gross domestic product. In this scenario, transnational corporations have increased the monopolistic control over global markets, millions of farmers have been dispossessed of their land, and millions of workers have been dispossessed of good jobs. Another essential feature of the financialization of capital is short-termism in business since finance has become decoupled from production and favoured instability. Indeed, one of the lessons learned after the 2008 global financial crisis is that inclusive growth is not compatible with global capital mobility, securitized finance, and the expansion of institutional investors within the shadow banking system (The Economist 2011).

All these things considered, what is the dark side in the examples of nudges related to the re-arrangement of healthy food in cafeteria lines, the encouragement to save for retirement by opting into a specified investment plan, the inclusion of notifications in smart-phone software to alert the user to their calorific intake?

Looking back, the transformation of a welfare state into a Libertarian Paternalist state is one of the crucial but not fully understood trends in politics.

Rationalism in politics

In the well-known article *Libertarian Paternalism Is Not an Oxymoron*, published in the *Chicago Law Review*, Sunstein and Thaler (2003, 26) state:

> A libertarian paternalist who is especially enthusiastic about free choice would be inclined to make it relatively costless for people to obtain their preferred outcomes. (Call this a *libertarian* paternalist.) By contrast, a libertarian paternalist who is especially confident of his welfare judgments would be willing to impose real costs on workers and consumers who seek to do what, in the paternalist's view, would not be in their best interests. (Call this a libertarian *paternalist.*)

In other words, Libertarian Paternalism is moderate because it lies on a *continuum* between anarchy and totalitarianism. Sunstein and Thaler (2003) clearly state that there is no alternative to paternalism. Due to the cognitive biases, governments need to guide people to make rational decisions in education, healthcare, savings, etc.

In Sunstein's 2016 book *The Ethics of Influence: Government in the Age of Behavioral Science* poses the question, "what are the ethical constraints on influence when it comes from government?" The short answer is: welfare, autonomy, dignity, and self-government. Individual autonomy should always be considered in relation to the outcomes that influence individual welfare and happiness. In summary, what matters is whether the benefits are substantial and if the damage (harm) to the individual's dignity and self-respect is minimal (Sunstein 2016). Therefore, the relevant issue refers to the welfare outcomes for each individual.

In accordance with Libertarian Paternalism, citizens trust the choice architect (government) that respects freedom itself as a value to protect (Thaler and Sunstein 2008, 242). Though human liberty can exist only within a system of norms, Sunstein (1996) argues that the key question is whether social norms can be obstacles to human autonomy and well-being. Social life cannot exist without norms since they affect the individual beliefs of harm and risk and make freedom possible. However, when norms are inadequate, society can face large difficulties and even collapse. Sunstein believes that norms can change and concludes that the government, as a choice architect, can have a role in establishing new norms. In this attempt, the advocates of Libertarian Paternalism address that opt-out options reduce the slippery-slope risk (Thaler and Sunstein 2008, 251).

Libertarian Paternalists neglect the cognitive biases of policymakers which can lead them to misunderstand or even ignore the longer-term costs of their policies. In view of the slippery-slope risk argument, Thaler and Sunstein (2008) respond to their critics by saying that the risk must be counted as a learning cost. In their opinion, even if not entirely satisfactory, the inclusion of opt-outs in contracts so as to preserve freedom is an improvement. Indeed, when opt-outs are unavailable, the slippery-slope risk argument can have some relevance. For instance, when considering health care, the authors advocate greater liberty of contract to sue the doctors if the patients prefer and to opt-out with the waiver if they want to reduce costs (Thaler and Sunstein 2008, 207–214). Here the nudges appear to be the rules that frame the decision making of individuals by default.

The ethical principles considered by Sunstein call for a reflection on the differences between classical liberalism and Libertarian Paternalism. Classical liberalism advocates that "we can all be free", in the larger context of the constitution of liberty rather than in the context of some rational utilitarian calculus of gains and costs. Indeed, the key guiding principles of classical liberalism are the recognition of the limits of human rationality and the social nature of men. The social world arises from human action and not from human design.

Classical liberals would certainly put in to question the Libertarian Paternalist state's legitimacy in a democratic context, since the principles of classical liberalism aim to defeat the growing state intrusion so as to protect individuals and society. The classical liberal triad – liberty, dignity, and individual responsibility – that builds the foundations of the moral character of liberal societies seems to be shaken by paternalist states whose interventions degrade the dignity and liberty of individuals.

The advocates of classical liberalism claim that current relations among individuals, norms, and the state are favouring a concept of citizenship associated to market rationality. Citizens are also being threatened by totalitarian and tyrannical governments, since "bureaucracies are the dominant means by which governments control and influence the daily lives of people through the world" (Scherrer 2006, 199). One of the current concerns refers to the medicalization of politics. In health systems, the coercion mechanisms masquerade as profit-seeking medical treatments. However, Thaler and Sunstein do not discuss the influence of special interests that may continually steer nudges. Policymakers may be influenced by supposedly neutral experts, special interests, as well as financial, moral, or ideological reasons.

Behind the Libertarian Paternalist proposal is the belief that the government, as a choice architect, can implement rationalist social engineering.

Indeed, Saint-Paul (2011) states that behavioural economics is the last bastion of rationalism in economic science. We can add that the normativity implications of behavioural economics have spread in the context of the predominance of modern rationalism in politics, which has roots in the Cartesian narrative. Indeed, although behavioural economics criticizes the concept of the rational, maximizing individual, its normative programme promotes the state as a rational agent (Glaeser 2004).

Michael Oakeshott (1991) developed a deep objection to rationalism in politics in that it is justified by aprioristic principles supported by the authority of reason. As the solution of problems does not consider circumstances and variety, it turns out to be uniform and based on an artificial rationalistic logic. In his perspective, the rationalist perspective in politics spread the belief that human actions can be delivered adequately through guidelines of explicit rules designed by a "rational" bureaucracy. This belief relies on a theoretical model of how society ought to behave in the context of freedom. What the philosopher argues is that rationalism in politics should be rejected since freedom cannot be imposed on people in accordance with some preconceived scheme.

Then, modern rationalism in politics believes in the power of reason to achieve true goals. Politics cannot be reduced to problem-solving techniques that are set in a *nudge continuum* that disregards the crucial distinction between private and public aims and practices (Whitman 2010).

All things consider, we can say that nudging is one of these problem-solving techniques that search for the best rational (and managerial) practices. Outside the laboratories, Libertarian Paternalists have great potential for facing the slippery-slope risk, as Rizzo and Whitman warned (2007, 2009a, 2009b).

Nudges and neoliberalism

The neoliberal governance of the self

Much of the commentary on neoliberal governance has focused on governance issues related to risk management, monetary policy, and weak regulation. However, the *social and political* dimensions of the global transformations have received little attention.

Changes in power relations and political configurations enhanced the rise of the self-regulated markets and the financialization of everyday life. Following the neoliberal orthodoxy, many developed and developing countries adopted a new economic agenda supported by certain interest groups and government technocrats committed to liberalization. Indeed, after the 1970s, new political alignments fostered substantial changes in global financial regulation. In the context of capital market liberalization and political ascendancy of finance capital, macroeconomic stability and fiscal prudence turned out to be primary policy objectives, while the social targets related to job creation and income redistribution were not favoured. Changes in state–market relations have supported a general disembedding of the economy from society and from democratic politics. In this setting, nudging appears to be implemented as a non-coercive government intervention.

Looking back, in the lectures at the Collège de France in 1978–1979, Foucault (2004) developed a reflection on the birth of biopolitics, where neoliberalism as a doctrine of political economy and a form of governmentality was highlighted. The French philosopher realized that neoliberalism was not only related to economics and governmental politics, but it represented a scheme for social reorganization and for reshaping the subjectivity (self) of individuals (McGuigan 2014). The neoliberal self should be consistent with "the recasting of identity in terms of flexibility, adaptability and instant transformation" (Elliot and Urry 2010, 7).

Mainly in the 1979 lectures, Foucault proposed the study of the neoliberal forms of government, after discussing the contributions of Adam Smith, David Hume, and Adam Ferguson to classical liberalism. While analysing the neoliberal governmentality, he focused on German postwar liberalism (Ordoliberals) and the liberalism of the Chicago School. While classical liberalism faces the problem of how to establish sufficient market freedoms within an existing state, the Ordoliberals put in to question how a state could be created on the basis of economic liberty. After the 1940s, the German school of thought rejected the principles and practices of the emergent welfare State. The OrdoLiberals claim that the constitution of the market depends on political interventions (Foucault 2004). In other words, the historical evolution of the capitalist system depends on the evolution of an economic-institutional set-up that can be changed politically (McGuigan 2014).

Like the Ordoliberals, the American neoliberalism of the Chicago School criticizes the growth of bureaucratic apparatuses and the threat to individual rights. For their advocates, the market serves as the organizational principle for the state and society, and they focus on the analysis of human actions oriented by the economic rationality (Foucault 2004). Their ideas call for a return to the *homo economicus* with the emphasis on the "responsibility" of rational individuals.

According to Foucault, the "responsibility" of rational individuals involves a process of adjustment and control – increasingly economic. Neoliberal governance refers to mechanisms of power that are understood as mechanisms of normalization in society. In other words, the "rational" subjects are the result of disciplinary power.

Foucault's analysis of neoliberalism shows that it is a political project that endeavours to create a social reality. Taking into account the political rationality of neoliberalism, it is a strategy that fosters the responsibility of individual subjects' for social risks, such as illness and unemployment. Social responsibility becomes a matter of personal provision. Indeed, the political rationality of neoliberalism enhances a reduction in welfare and security systems in order to favour the so called personal responsibility and self-care (Garland 1996).

Indeed, nudging has an effect in terms of (self-)regulation. While the principles of neoliberalism encourage individuals to be rational, the individuals themselves have to assume responsibility for their cognitive biases and the outcomes of their choices. The neoliberal governance of self-care relies on the rationale of the two selves of Kahneman's dual system. Governing people involves techniques of nudging through which the relation between the selves may be modified. The neoliberal governance of nudging turns out to be a form of government management that is implemented through the framing of choice-making by a government technocracy. In truth, the power mechanisms behind nudging become a technical question rather than a political one. Therefore, behind the Libertarian Paternalism proposal of Thaler and Sunstein there are implicit forms of political power and processes of subjectification.

Nudges and pension savings

According to Thaler and Sunstein (2008), if there is an obesity problem, nudges may influence people to change their life style; if there is a climate change problem, nudging people may change behaviours related to consumption and recycling. They also argue in favour of nudging workers to make rational decisions regarding their pension savings. The implementation approach of behavioural economics relies on the individuals: they are the cause and the solution for the economic and social problems. However, they should be helped by governments.

Halpern (2015) highlights recent changes in pension savings – such as in the UK, United States, and New Zealand – that utilised nudging which was aimed to enhance auto-enrolment in pension plans. Taking into account this example, we can ask: what is really the dark side in the behavioural policy interventions related to pension savings?

Financial deregulation, the redefinition of the role of the nation-states and pension reforms have fostered the expansion of pension funds where individuals may participate in mandatory or quasi-mandatory plans and/or one or several voluntary plans (OECD 2009). Ten years after the crisis, one relevant question relies on how the neoliberal governance may influence the savings and incomes of older people and future generations.

Many governments in OECD countries have been committed to structural reforms in labour markets and pension plans. After the 2008 global financial crisis, OECD countries implemented cuts in public-sector wages, cuts in social welfare, investment projects reduction, expenditure cuts and tax increases, changes in retirement age, and changes in pension payments.

Between 2007 and 2017, pension assets in the OECD area kept growing and amounted to US$43.4 trillion in 2017. Those pension assets are unevenly distributed among world regions and across countries since there is a concentration in the OECD area. In 2017, the largest amounts of pension assets were located in the United States (US$16.2 trillion), followed by the United Kingdom (US$2.9 trillion), Australia (US$ 1.7 trillion), the Netherlands (US$ 1.6 trillion) and Canada (US$ 1.4 trillion). However, the size of private pension systems shrank in some countries where pension reforms adopted the pay-as-you-go system (Madi 2018).

Nowadays, there are different types of pension plans (OECD 2018). In a mandatory pension plan, either:

1) employers setup a plan for their employees;
2) employees contribute to a state funded pension scheme; or
3) employees contribute to a private pension fund of their choice.

In contrast, in a quasi-mandatory plan, employers need to set up a pension plan on behalf of labour agreements set with their employees. In some countries, there are automatic enrolment programmes at the national level where employees have the option to opt out of the plan under certain conditions. Taking this scenario into account, neoliberal governance has favoured retirement plans that privilege the use of defined contribution (DC) pension plans (for example, the United States). In a DC pension plan, the employer, the employee, or both make contributions on a regular basis in individual accounts.

Behind nudging people to make rational decisions in their saving pension plans, what is really happening is that, ten years after the global crisis, the funding ratio of occupation defined benefit (DB) pension plans is below their pre-financial crisis levels in most of the OECD reporting countries. Many factors drove the evolution of the funding ratio and the asset-liability management of DB pension plans:

1) low interest rates,
2) the composition of assets,

3) the number of members and their level of wages,
4) benefits paid,
5) the age structure of members,
6) the aggregate price level.

(Madi 2018)

All things considered, a key current trend can be highlighted: a shift to DC pension plans. Therefore, behind nudging people to make rational decisions on savings, there are hidden matters: the declining funding ratios of pension funds below 100 per cent and their financial sustainability. Nudging people cannot avoid the underfunding of pension funds. Financial regulators need to monitor the evolution of funding ratios in order to protect members and sponsors.

Nudges and employability

Employment has historically undergone significant qualitative changes. These issues have been long debated in the pages of sociology, management, and behavioural studies. Taking into account the development of behavioural economics, its normative suggestion has focused nudging workers to influence behavioural changes. It is supposed that the change of behaviours will increase the chance of getting a job, or even to encourage workers to be more productive and efficient (Halpern 2015). What is hidden behind the proposal of nudging workers is that small individual behavioural changes are drivers to employability.

The relation between employability, labour flexibility, and the current financially-oriented accumulation pattern are indeed complex. According to Standing (2011) the concept of labour market flexibility has several dimensions:

1) Wage flexibility generally means downwards adjustments in nominal incomes.
2) Employment flexibility means downsizing strategies with reduction in employment security and protection.
3) Job flexibility means changes inside job structures.

Employment flexibility involves changes in the length of the working week, the adoption of part-time working, temporary employment contracts, outsourcing, and home-working. Job flexibility aims to increase efficiency and refers to multi-tasking, just-in-time-production, quality management, and team working. In this scenario, new skills and competences of individual employees are required while precariousness and informalization of workers increase. Kalleberg and Vallas (2018, 2) add that "Precarious work has made the availability as well as the quality of jobs more risky and uncertain".

Even before the 2008 global financial crisis, most economies fell short of creating jobs. Downsizing strategies and new technologies put pressure downward on the rate of employment and sharply increased the demand for skilled workers. In this scenario, feelings of anxiety and stress have increased among workers (Wichert 2002).

According to the doctrine of self-regulated markets, a flexible labour market would avoid rigidities and/or restrictions, such as labour regulations, in order to enhance the creation of jobs to the full employment level. Looking back, in the mid-1930s, John Maynard Keynes (1936 (1964)) rejected this doctrine and gave an explanation for the capitalist fundamental social problem: *involuntary unemployment*. Against the classical economists that defend the self-regulated markets, Keynes proposed that the government should intervene in the market economy in order to decrease the level of involuntary unemployment. The key element in the government intervention strategy should be the management of aggregate demand – the primary driver of economic expansion.

To explain involuntary unemployment, Keynes focused his theory on the main features of a monetary economy where uncertainty pervades the decision-making process. In *The General Theory of Employment* (1936 (1964)), he argues that employers make decisions about the amount of labour that they would hire based on uncertain profit expectations. On behalf of the uncertainty about the future, businessmen could postpone investment decisions and search for alternatives of wealth management. Then, the level of employment not only depends on the expected profits in the markets of goods and services but also on the expected returns in the financial markets.

The linkages between finance and unemployment are "a prominent feature of neoliberalism" (Duménil and Lévy 2007). In this new scenario, new rules of corporate finance fostered the growth of institutional investors – such as pension funds or private equity firms – in business as relevant shareholders. The drive to increase the shareholders' short-term profits favours mergers and acquisitions, and fosters financial bubbles. The aims of global investors have relied on a whole range of management and financial innovations that have been described by Froud et al. (2006) and include inter-corporate sell-offs, spin-offs, acquisitions by leveraged buyouts (LBOS), and management buyouts (MBOs).

In this scenario, corporate governance has privileged downsizing and distribution of short-term profits. Workers are fired if short-term profits decrease, and those who remained employed are responsible for carrying the burden of increasing productivity. In practice, employers aim to hire contingent workers in order to reduce costs (Polivka and Nardone 1989, 12).

The downsizing "obsession" reveals the interrelation between financial power, corporate governance, and labour flexibility that submits livelihoods to huge losses in terms of employment and income. The overall outcomes have not been socially acceptable since managerial restructuring strategies put pressure on the elimination of social protections for all workers. At the heart of our argument is that the financially-led accumulation pattern involves *social* relations driven by profit and competition. Then, the clear cut between investors and managers favours flexible labour relations and the end of jobs "as we know it" (Bauman 2000, 147).

Rationalization and flexibility happen to increase uncertainties, inequalities, and inhuman conditions of living around the world. Instead of improving individual well-being, nudging workers aims to boost productivity and efficiency, and feed profits.

Dark nudges

Nudges and inequality

Ulrich Beck and Elisabeth Beck-Gernsheim (2001/2002) have addressed that the neoliberal-self is condemned to freedom and lonely responsibility. What factors contribute to the circumstances under which the neoliberal-self is situated in relation to the transformations in production, employment, and consumption?

Since the 1970s, the expansion of *financial capital* has increased control over the structural forms necessary for the continuing cycles of valorisation of productive capital, thanks to the centralized money at disposal. Different growth models overwhelmed this global scenario. While some countries have presented a consumption-driven growth model fuelled by credit, generally followed by current account deficits, other countries have shown an export-driven growth model, mainly characterized by modest consumption growth and large current account surpluses (Stockhammer 2009). The growth of financial assets, generated by the new debt cycle, included increasing and sophisticated risk-management practices. This financial expansion also proved to subordinate the pace of investment to financial commitments. In spite of differences in the growth pattern, the finance-led accumulation regime has presented some distinctive features.

A redefinition of the role of the state justified privatization and deregulation in all product markets, as well as in the labour and financial markets. Another relevant change has been the redefinition of labour and working conditions that affected income distribution. The evolution of the capitalist relations of production reveals changing labour organizing principles to cope with the dictates of increasing capital mobility: automatic production control, redefinition of tasks in the context of transformations in the varieties of capitalist management towards new kinds of control, job rotation, and suppression of skilled workers. Attacks on labour unions or the diminishing organizational strength of collective demands need to be underlined. The overall changes strengthened private and public debt and further social inequalities.

After the 2008 global financial crisis, central banks and treasuries were not exempt from private pressures to prevent a collapse of domestic financial systems. In this scenario, the implementation of austerity programmes required new macroeconomic guidelines that certainly affected livelihoods. Austerity programmes subordinate the whole policy decision process that turns out to look for the realignment of relative prices (mainly real wages) and further structural reforms (mainly in the public sector and the labour market). The increasing popularity of nudging coincides with the spread of programmes of fiscal austerity that have penalized the poor, while social inequality has increased.

Fiscal austerity aims at obtaining a surplus, after tax increases and expenditure cuts. In the scenario of macroeconomic and financial stabilization, changes in expectations on economic growth dampen future levels of investment, consumption, and employment. Therefore, fiscal austerity may be a risky long-term strategy as a tighter fiscal policy certainly results in even weaker economic growth rates and higher public debt/GDP rates. In addition, under high uncertainty, the expansion of productive capacity might be postponed. In this scenario, income inequality puts a downward pressure on the levels of households' consumption that have become increasingly dependent on credit, not only on mortgages but also on consumer loans, such as credit cards.

Fiscal austerity has been associated with furthering labour market flexibility. Taking into consideration the dynamics of current labour markets, employability seems to be conditioned to private strategies that aim for cost reductions, labour flexibility, and efficiency targets. The labour market becomes a key variable in macroeconomic policies based on austerity programmes that favour the reduction of the relative unit of labour costs. Wage cuts may prove to be devastating, not only socially and politically, but economically as well. Longer working hours, job destruction, turnover, outsourcing, workforce displacement, job reduction, and loss of rights are part of the spectrum of management practices that emerge from the austerity guidelines.

This scenario, characterized by precarious jobs, enhances the vulnerability of workers, mainly young people and women. As a matter of fact, the recent dynamics of the global labour market has reinforced the precariousness of women's employment and working conditions. Among other issues, the recent global highlights (ILO 2016) about the participation of women in the labour markets are listed below:

- Unemployment: women are more likely to be unemployed than men, with global unemployment rates of 5.5 per cent for men and 6.2 per cent for women.
- Informal work: in 2015, a total of 586 million women were own-account or contributing family workers. Many working women remain in occupations that are more likely to consist of informal work arrangements.
- Wage and salaried jobs: moreover, 52.1 per cent of women and 51.2 per cent of men in the labour market are wage and salaried workers.
- Jobs and occupations by economic sectors: globally, the services sector has overtaken agriculture as the sector that employs the highest number of people. In the period between 1995 and 2015, the participation of women in the services sector increased from 41.1 per cent to 61.5 per cent.
- High-skilled occupations: high-skilled occupations expanded faster for women than for men in emerging economies where there is a gender gap in high-skilled employment in women's favour.
- Part-time jobs: globally, women represent less than 40 per cent of total employment, but make up 57 per cent of those working on a part-time basis.
- Hours of work: across the global labour scenario, one fourth of women in employment (25.7 per cent) work more than 48 hours a week, mainly in Eastern, Western, and Central Asia, where almost half of women employed work more than 48 hours a week.
- Gender wage gap: globally, on average women earn 77 per cent of what men earn.

The 2008 global crisis outcomes seem to have increased the challenges for accessing better jobs and reducing gender inequalities. The policy responses to the crisis could not avoid putting pressure on women that suffered workforce adjustments in industrial manufacturing. Otherwise, the expansion of female formal jobs in trade and services activities fosters precarious jobs, mainly based on short-term contracts with low earnings.

Indeed, although women have been increasing their participation rate in the labour market in the last decades, they work in more precarious occupations. In addition to women's current challenges in the labour market, the increasing weight of unpaid work is more likely when women become unemployed and return to their homes and take more responsibility for housework than men, or because the loss of family income makes it impossible to support the remuneration of domestic workers. Gender-differentiated time-use patterns are affected by many factors, including: household composition (age and gender composition of household members), seasonal considerations, regional and geographic factors, availability of infrastructure, and social services. However, social norms, that is to say, what others believe and are really doing, also play an important role both in defining, and sustaining the status quo in the gender division of labour.

In view of this scenario, the relevant concerns are *who imposes the costs* of the governance of self-care and *in which context* are they imposed. Austerity programmes reveal the deep transformations in the relation between state and citizens. Many governments have disappointed their citizens after restructuring social policies and changing pension plans in a context of higher informality in labour markets and low rates of economic growth.

The increasing popularity of nudging coincides with the spread of programmes of fiscal austerity that have penalized the poor, while efficiency and effectiveness in the public sector turn out to be social targets. At a time when governments face deeps budgetary constraints, nudges are considered cost effective and behavioural initiatives are organized through a variety of public–private partnerships to promote behavioural changes, that is to say, more profits (Pykett et al. 2014, 97). For example, the UK Nudge Unit was reorganized as a "profit-making joint venture" (Halpern 2015). Looking back, in the late 1950s, Vance Packard's classic *The Hidden Persuaders* (1957) showed how corporations, retailers, and modern media manipulate the consumers through the subliminal messages of advertising that aimed at influencing decision-making processes. Also psychologists, such as Harlow Gale and Walter Dill Scott, studied how psychological insights and deliberately manipulative techniques in advertising can influence decisions. Indeed, human emotions, desires, and insecurities have been exploited by consumer capitalism. The relevant topic is whether nudges are being shaped by corporate interests.

Therefore, what matters is who imposes the costs of the governance of self-care and in which context these costs are imposed. Taking into consideration the unemployed, the real nature of the governance of self-care has been exposed by the complaints of offended jobseekers (Malik

2013). For example, the UK Nudge Unit introduced a practice that required applicants for unemployment benefits to complete an online survey that gathered information about personality features to help in finding a job. The survey results aimed at making recommendations to the applicants to change their behaviour and address their problem of "worklessness" (Cromby and Willis 2014, 242). After this, many people condemned this nudging as a lie, as indeed it was (Stone 2013).

As Fitoussi (2005) has claimed in his analysis on the current social and economic challenges, when taking into account the trade-off between efficient behavioural economic policies and social justice, the former ones are only possible in a society that tolerates more inequalities.

Nudges, ethics, and democracy

Throughout the last forty years, most governments around the world supported the long-run process of neoliberal reforms that turned out to be characterized by the financialization of the capitalist economy. In this historical scenario, monopoly-finance capital became increasingly dependent on bubbles that, both in credit and capital markets, proved to be globally the sources of endogenous financial fragility. This process was reinforced, in a vicious circle, by a concentration of income, wealth, and power. By negatively influencing labour and working conditions, it became increasingly difficult for effective demand to reach the level of full employment of gross national product. In response to this situation, banking and credit policies, also supported by governments and supranational institutions, were enabling consumers to expand their spending through increasing debt. While public spending on social and infrastructural objectives was severely restricted, it expanded in other areas, sustaining the income and the demand of powerful groups.

In truth, global trends in capital accumulation and competition have shaped a scenario where practices in corporate finance favoured mergers and acquisitions aimed to increase the shareholder value by means of a "clash of rationalization". In this context, competitiveness and productivity have been put together in an attempt to promote higher business performance. In a scenario of expansion of capital markets and the emergence of new business strategies, investments that are fixed for society turn out to be liquid for investors. Today, the dominance of a culture based on short-term profits has major implications that go far beyond the narrow confines of the financial markets. The costs of this business model fall disproportionately on society because of the commitment to *liquidity*. As Keynes warned in his analysis on the monetary theory of production,

> Thus the professional investor is forced to concern himself with the anticipation of impending changes, in the news or in the atmosphere, of the kind by which experience shows that the mass psychology of the market is most influenced. This is the inevitable result of investment markets organized with a view to so-called "liquidity". Of the maxims of orthodox finance none, surely, is more anti-social than the fetish of liquidity, the doctrine that it is a positive virtue on the part of investment institutions to concentrate their resources upon the holding of "liquid" securities. It forgets that there is no such thing as liquidity of investment for the community as a whole.
>
> (Keynes 1936 (1964: 155)

Indeed, the financial conception of investment gained ground in the context where financial innovations aimed to achieve short-term profits with lower capital requirements. Managers and owners of firms focused on financial gains often based on speculative shifts of shareholder values. Changes in corporate ownership, through waves of mergers and acquisitions, created new business models where companies, while highly powerful and concentrated, turned out to be simply bundles of financial assets and liabilities to be traded. Hence, current corporate governance came to have the privilege of mobility, liquidity, and short-term profits based on high levels of debt.

Moreover, the OECD (2015) report puts in to question the complexity of the current investment chain due to:

1) cross-investments among institutional investors;
2) increased complexity in equity market structure and trade practices; and
3) an increase in outsourcing of ownership and asset management functions.

In this scenario, deleterious economic and social outcomes have involved a trend to "downsize and distribute", that is to say, a trend to restructure, reduce costs, and focus on short-term gains. In practice this has meant plant displacement and closures, outsourcing of jobs, and changing employment conditions in the global markets. Therefore, in this scenario, there has been an increase in precarious jobs, technological unemployment, and informality, in addition to fragile conditions of social protection (Stiglitz 2015). First, labour-saving technologies have reduced the demand for many middle-class and blue-collar jobs. Second, globalization has created a global marketplace, confronting expensive unskilled workers with cheap unskilled workers overseas and favouring outsourcing practices. Third, social changes have also played a role in the labour market changes, such as the decline of unions. Four, political decisions are influenced by the top 1 per cent who favour policies that increase income inequality.

Then, in the new millennium, the proliferation of financial assets, with unstable economic growth, has given way to widespread precarious jobs, income gaps, and weaker welfare programmes in the context of the self-regulated capitalism. The same policies that have obliterated social services and kept labour cheap have supported the expansion of short-termism and new global business models in the context of deregulated capitalism. All things considered, the onset of the twenty-first century represents a new political age overwhelmed by the violation of democratic ideals of political equality and social peace. Indeed, democracy has been allowing for election to office but not to power. And, as a consequence, policy makers might give priority to their sponsors instead of the needs of citizens – decent work and income equality (Lima and Madi 2016).

All these trends reveal issues of current power, politics, and economics in a social context where democratic institutions are being threatened. Taking into consideration this setting, nudging as a politics of self-governance, relies on the transfer of power from democratic institutions to technocratic institutions. This is justified by the target: to make rational choices and individuals happier, people need "a helping hand" to be rational and exercise self-control. It is worth remembering the words of Sunstein and Thaler (2003, 1159):

> Equipped with an understanding of behavioral findings of bounded rationality and bounded self-control, libertarian paternalists should attempt to steer people's choices in welfare-promoting directions without eliminating freedom of choice. It is also possible to show how a libertarian paternalist might select among the possible options and to assess how much choice to offer.

This proposal does not seem to take into account the global economic, social, and political challenges and their impacts on the future of democracy. In his recent book *Can Democracy Survive Global Capitalism?* Robert Kuttner (2018) argues that the globalization of capital has affected the very foundation of a healthy democracy since financial capital has subordinated social dynamics to the demands of speculative private capital, instead of attending social needs. The main concern is: do current economic and social trends stimulate disillusioned voters to support Libertarian Paternalism? Answering this question not only involves critical thinking on economic policies but also a reflection on ethical challenges of nudging. As Henry Farrell warns, subtle nudges, properly constructed, are too nuanced and too cleverly hidden to escape notice and objection. Addressing these challenges involve critical thinking on contemporary policy alternatives, considering that power, knowledge, and ethical issues are intertwined.

Many contributions have analysed the hidden ethics of nudging. From the liberal standpoint, Becker (2007) calls for a comparison between Hayek, who believed in a learning process that leads individuals to improve their choices, and Libertarian Paternalists, who emphasize the permanent conflict among the double self within a person.

From another perspective, in the book *The Manipulation of Choice: Ethics and Libertarian Paternalism*, Mark White (2013) makes reference to the ethical problem of giving governmental authorities the power to use information about people's cognitive biases to help people make rational choices. Indeed, White argues that one of the possible outcomes of these practices is the manipulation of individuals by government that use their coercive power to change the choice framing and exploit cognitive biases. For him, the unjustified presumption of nudging is that policymakers will favour the choices that people would make if they were well informed and unbiased. In addition to the knowledge problem, there is the concern that policy makers may impose their own values or judgments as technical and neutral decisions. For White, Libertarian Paternalism denies individual autonomy as the principle that determines the individual interests and actions since the manipulation of choices promotes the interest imposed by the technocracy (White 2013, 92). In the light of this concern, White states that the hidden ethics of nudging favors a rational approach to policy making that mainly exploits cognitive biases instead of promoting the development of cognitive skills and individual autonomy.

Years before, Jonhathan Klick (2010) drew attention to the idea that neoliberal policy-making is highly influenced by lobbyists and congressional staffers, whose interests do not seem to rely on social welfare.

The dark side of nudges as a behavioural policy is whether data-driven nudges are being shaped by privatization programmes and corporate interests.

Digital nudges and surveillance

Nudges, discipline and control

When analysing the philosophical justification for the use of nudge, Libertarian Paternalists recall the seminal significance of J. S. Mill's *On Liberty* (1859 (2011)), where the harm principle refers to the appropriate limits of government intervention in people's lives. For Mill, children and the mentally ill have to be protected from themselves. The average citizen, capable of reason, however, should at the most be subjected to interventions aimed to balance out any lack in information.

However, as Anne Brunon-Ernst (2016) explains, the contribution of the British philosopher and legal reformer Jeremy Bentham seems to be more appropriate to understand the Libertarian Paternalist proposal. For Bentham, legality relies on a system of laws so that citizens can respond to them rationally. At the beginning of the industrial revolution, Bentham's contribution to the debate on indirect legislation advocates that freedom in a political society depends on a legal system that creates obligations and rights. In this setting, the government, as legislator, knows and guides individual behaviours toward beneficial goals for the community as a whole.

Bentham's proposals were embedded in a utilitarian world-view of pleasure and pain where the behaviour of individuals was attached to an "invisible chain". It is crucial to highlight the manner in which Bentham expected the individuals to modify their behaviour without coercion. According to him, the habit of watching and judging others in society is the best way to learn self-discipline.

In the context of the emergence of the capitalist industrial society, Bentham condemned the old model of punishment based on public executions and infliction of physical pain. The project of a prison that he named *Panopticon* – literally meaning all-seeing – was related to the most cost-efficient model of punishment, oriented not only to reform convicted criminals but also to prevent crimes being committed. This project was based on some assumptions:

- the omnipresence of the inspector ensured by his total invisibility, and
- the universal visibility and constant observation of the objects of surveillance.

The Panopticon scheme started out as a Russian factory under the supervision of Bentham's brother Samuel. In one of his letters from Russia, Bentham suggested that this scheme could be adopted in all kinds of institutions. In his own words:

> No matter how different, or even opposite the purpose: whether it be that of punishing the incorrigible, guarding the insane, reforming the vicious, confining the suspected, employing the idle, maintaining the helpless, curing the sick, instructing the willing in any branch of industry, or training the rising race in the path of education: in a word, whether it be applied to the purposes of perpetual prisons in the room of death, or prisons for confinement before trial, or penitentiary-

> houses, or houses of correction, or work-houses, or manufactories, or mad-houses, or hospitals, or schools.
>
> (Bentham 1843: 40)

In the Panopticon scheme, the power over people, that is to say the power as domination, refers to the spatial organization of different categories of inmates in order to observe them, to punish and to discipline those who violate the rules. On the other hand, the power exercised over oneself, that is to say, the power as discipline, refers to the self-discipline of inmates who know that they are under constant surveillance. Therefore, the Panopticon makes coercion mostly unnecessary except in some rare cases of disobedience. In sum, it is supposed that the permanent visibility of individuals would prevent them from certain types of behaviour since Panopticon as a dispositive might end up exercising power over them without any coercion.

The recent interest in Bentham's investigation of alternative forms of government practices emerged on behalf of Foucault's analysis of biopolitics (Manokha 2018). In the book *Discipline and Punish*, Foucault (1995) used the example of Bentham's Panopticon prison as a metaphor to examine its relevance for the analysis of modern means of surveillance:

> Hence the major effect of the Panopticon: to induce in the inmate a state of conscious and permanent visibility that assures the automatic functioning of power. So to arrange things that the surveillance is permanent in its effects, even if it is discontinuous in its action; that the perfection of power should tend to render its actual exercise unnecessary; that this architectural apparatus should be a machine for creating and sustaining a power relation independent of the person who exercises it; in short, that the inmates should be caught up in a power situation of which they are themselves the bearers.
>
> (p. 201)

Surveillance has particularly grown with the rise of modernity and of a centralized bureaucratic state. The key, specific feature of modern power mechanisms is that they aim at producing a process of domination marked by subjection and its effects. The disciplinary power may be exercised by the action of micro-powers present in the totality of the social space. In the last decade, the turning point of this disciplinary power trend is the use of behavioural data that reveals the deep interconnections among surveillance states, personal devices, and Big Data.

Within this scenario, Foucault (2004) also highlights the importance of experts who create scientific truths about normal standards and anomalies or deviances.

A relevant topic refers to the impacts of modern surveillance on governmentality in Western democratic societies. Foucault deploys the concept of government or "governmentality" as a guideline to stimulate a critical discussion on modern neo-liberalism. Indeed, in the context of neoliberalism, there is a new type of power, based on the regulation and surveillance of individuals, which crosses all apparatus and institutions. Permanent vigilance and observation become an essential component of the techniques of power disseminated in multiple institutional forms. Neoliberalism as a socio-cultural process provokes changes in modes of governance, and subjectivities and behaviours. In this context, there certainly is a resonance between the developments in behavioural economics and the transformations in modern surveillance. In accordance with Foucault's analysis of neoliberalism, nudging people enhances a kind of disciplinary power based on norms and normalization standards that aim to exercise control on individuals.

Nudges, neoliberal (managerial) policies, and Big Data

Economic conditions are constantly changing. Today, our generation is confronted with the outcomes of contemporary globalization that is a complex and multifaceted process, characterized by new markets, new actors, and new rules. Globalization has produced many changes in our economy, society, culture, and politics. Deep pressures to conform to new standards of behaviour, such as efficiency and competitive performance have forced individuals and communities not only to rethink values and practices but also to rebalance tradition and change. In this setting, the current neoliberal politics of nudges has been increasingly prevalent in current economic thinking and policies. In this context, changing behaviours come to mean "survival" in the face of the outcomes of the neoliberal capitalism that is threatening the earthly life, human societies, and cultures. Therefore, nudges, subjectification and self-responsibility are closely interlinked in the context of neoliberalism.

Nudge as a policy recommendation seeks to enhance the cognitive ability of individuals and communities to cope with market uncertainties. James Brasset and Christopher Holmes (2016) present a literature review on the neoliberal (and managerial) policies characterized as a set of governance techniques aimed to manage uncertainty and achieve the adaptation of individuals and communities to global changes. Taking into account the dynamics of the labour markets, for example, the evolution of unemployment is understood as the results from the "unsuitable" or "inappropriate" behaviour of workers. Then, the neoliberal (managerial) policies have turned out to enhance the adaptation of the behaviour of workers to the "market discipline". Those adaptive strategies focused on the attempt to rationally face uncertainties and risks.

Behind nudges and the recommendations to change behaviours, there has been a re-distribution of economic and political power among states, businessmen, investors, and workers. In the context of globalized markets, individuals and communities face many challenges because of the deep transformations in the trends of income and wealth inequality. In this setting, corporate ownership and strategies changed after waves of mergers and acquisitions. As a result companies are considered to be bundles of financial assets and liabilities to be traded in order to obtain short-term profits (Madi, 2018). In this setting, employability seems to be conditioned to the spectrum of management alternatives aimed at cost reduction. Then, workers turned out to redefine their skills, become informal entrepreneurs or migrate, among other examples of the current worldwide changes in their livelihoods.

All things considered, the nudge discourse offers new "frames" that rely on the *diagnosis* of cognitive biases and the *prognosis* of government intervention that suggests a solution to help individuals making rational judgments and decisions (Pyysiäinen et al. 2017). In the light of behavioural economics, nudges can re-frame the decision context in order to achieve rational decisions in the management of unemployment, health, education, and retirement plans, among others.[2]

Halpern (2015, 179) claims that shaping better nudges requires better data. In his view, a powerful type of nudge, can be designed with the developments of data science. People's habits and actions turn out to be valuable data. In Halpern's own words (2015, 183), "you should be in no doubt about one thing using 'big' and behavioural data to tailor and shape nudges is potentially very powerful."

Behind nudging people, there is the technocratic and/or corporatization of governance, as well as the relevant issue of surveillance. In truth, surveillance turns out to be a key word in the attempt to understand the current concerns around the outcomes of nudges.

What does surveillance mean and what are the implications of the practices of surveillance states?

The cultural dimension of surveillance capitalism influences the construction of subjectivities that support the neoliberal social order (Monohan 2017, 202). The fact that a precise goal of many government behavioural interventions is not established in advance, but it results from experiments that work, means that nudges have a kind of flexibility that put in to question the values that are being considered. The aims of nudging people may derive from multidimensional analysis of big data in unseen ways by the public who is not aware of the kinds of "profiles, predictions, prescriptions, and proscriptions" that are being generated in support of their guidance through nudges (Klauser and Albrechtslund

2014, 274). Today, the datafication of society enables different forms of government and corporate surveillance that combines physical and digital practices with the development of new information and communication technology.[3] Power techniques and forms of knowledge are intertwined and one of the main concerns is how surveillance, profiling, and discrimination restrict privacy and freedom (Kitchin et al. 2017, 20).

Then, the drive for further government interventions and the drive for more statistics are intertwined. The expansion of governmental activity in the gathering and disseminating of statistics in the last decades is certainly related to the similar expansion of surveillance techniques aimed at prescribing an appropriate behaviour for the society (Loewenstein and Haisley 2006). In this scenario, digital nudges involve practices of control, mediated by new technologies and computerized systems for "data gathering, data transfer and data analysis" (Klauser and Albrechtslund 2014, 277). Digital nudges have already being used in social security administration. Social media and e-health apps are feeding health insurers with "free" data. The aim of gathering information about race, gender, level of education, and daily habits is to obtain patterns of behaviour that can be re-framed. Behind the so called democratization of the access to internet services, there are algorithms … and nudges!

In the context of Big Data, individuals cannot be fully aware of the implications of the use of personal and cross information. The self-management of privacy, through consent regimes, is another example of how the neoliberal project produces new subjectivities. In Gordon Hulls's view, the so called privacy self-management "not only completely fails to protect privacy, but … it does so in a way that encourages adherence to several core neoliberal techniques of power" (Hull 2015, 90). In this setting, the economic power of transnational entities may influence the management of data derived from the operation of sensors, meters, and survey responses. As Hull warns, the (re)framing of choices becomes naturalized while individual "true" preferences are oriented to expand the global markets and profits (Hull 2015, 96).

Indeed, the new surveillance practices in health, education, and finance, among other sectors, manage data-flows that aim to develop rational actions by conditioning individual behaviour with subtle and subliminal messages, incentives, and opt-out options oriented to profitable outcomes. In education and health, for example, austerity programmes, Big Data and nudges have become interrelated. In a subtle way, this setting has re-framed the decisions of many parents about schools for their children under the myth of being *free to choose*. Behind austerity programmes and discretionary spending, nudging people has spread "the best (managerial) practices that work" in the public sector. As we have already claimed, the redefinition of the role of the state requires more data.

Recalling Karl Polanyi's conceptualization of the commodification of labour, land, and money in market societies, we can say that current surveillance practices reveal the commodification of behaviour. The centrality of the market entails that "Nothing must be allowed to inhibit the formation of markets, nor must incomes be permitted to be formed otherwise than through sales" (Polanyi 1944 (1971), 69). In other words, labour, land, money, and we can add evidence-based behaviour, turn out to be a commodity and are produced for sale. As the commodity fiction proves to be the vital organizing process, the self-regulated markets demand the institutional separation of society into economic and political spheres, that is to say, in the market society, the social relations are embedded in the economy rather than the economy embedded in social relations.

Other voices have recently spread their concerns about the future of Western societies. Harvard Professor Shoshana Zuboff (2015) analyses the main features of surveillance capitalism, invented by Google in 2001 and fostered by the dynamics of the self-regulated markets and the security policies after the attack on the World Trade Centre Towers. For Zuboff (2019), behavioural data is at the core of the concerns about the survival of democracy. She also states that, as surveillance capitalism aims to achieve behavioural modification on a global scale, it erodes democracy from within. Individual autonomy, moral judgment, and critical thinking are necessary for a democratic society. Moreover, democracy is also eroded from without, as surveillance capitalism enhances an unprecedented concentration in economic, political power and knowledge. Taking into account this background, digital nudges may be powered by vast amounts of data through proprietary technological systems and networks.

Another relevant contribution to the debate has been developed by Suzanne Mettler (2009) who argues that current conservative governance may lead to weaker citizenship. Mettler argues that for a democratic government to be "of the people, by the people, for the people", citizens should be able to have a clear view of the practices of their governments. The real concern is that citizens may remain uninformed and without real agency.

Taking into account the spread of nudges, Farrell (2017) addresses that the indirect attempts to guide our choices and behaviour are undermining the very core of democracy as nudging people assumes that individual choices can rely on the expertise of unelected technocrats. For Farrell, *nudgeocracy* is an outcome of Thaler and Sunstein's economic arguments that might lead to arbitrary and totalitarianism. In his view, the hidden side of *nudgeocracy* relies on the relevance of unelected technocrats who can re-frame and manipulate the behaviour of citizens. By avoiding dialogue and diversity in policy decision-making, the politics of nudges attacks the core of Western democracies and turns out to be other name for coercion (Farrell and Shalizi 2011).

In sum, nudges and the culture of control cannot be dissociated from the current political challenges.

Conclusion

The long-run process of financial expansion that turned out to be characterized as the "financialization" of the capitalist economy enhanced the expansion of monopoly-finance capital that became increasingly dependent on credit and financial bubbles (Foster 2009). Market deregulation, the financialization of corporate strategies, and labour flexibility can be associated with the construction of neoliberal governance. In this scenario, the spread of nudges is at its core of a set of complex economic, social, and political interrelations. Therefore, a critical perspective toward Libertarian Paternalism involves the understanding of hidden forms of power and processes of subjectivation.

The neoliberal governance of self-care (or neoliberal governance of the self) relies on DPTs, especially the one elaborated by Kahneman (2011). According to him, the distinction between *econs* and *humans* rejects the concept of *homo economicus* related to the neoclassical theory. The human brain functions in ways that refer to a distinction between two kinds of thinking: automatic thinking and reflective (rational) thinking, and Kahneman called these ways of thinking System 1 and System 2, respectively. His Dual Process Cognitive Theory tries to explain why human beings systematically deviate from rational decisions.

According to the Libertarian Paternalist' discourse of (re-)framing decisions, individuals are free to make choices, but they need help to be rational. On behalf of their dual psychological system, people cannot systematically pursue free choices based on rationally calculated preferences. The political rationality of neoliberalism calls for the relevance of System 2, the rational one in Kahneman's theoretical contribution. Rational calculation is fuelled by the "neoliberal" framing that calls for personal responsibility and self-care.

Shedding light on the contributions on Bentham's Panapticon and Foucault's biopolitics, this chapter illuminated a vast set of effects of nudges on the regulation and control of human life. As George Orwell told us in his dystopian vision of a society based on a state-based control, *1984*, totalitarianism not only requires citizens to act in accordance with the commands of the state but also requires citizens to believe in those commands.

Nowadays, nudges are part of the neoliberal governance and their spread raise concerns about economic inequality, technocracy, surveillance, and the future of democracy. The greatest challenge is to better understand the dark side of nudges.

Notes

1 Despite the critiques elaborated by Yeung (2012), among others.
2 On this topic, see Barnett et al. (2008). Dean (1995) analysed the rationale of the individual management of unemployment.
3 On this topic, see Galič et al. (2017).

References

Barnett, C., Clarke, N., Cloke, P., and Malpass, A. (2008). The elusive subjects of neo-liberalism: Beyond the analytics of governmentality. *Cultural Studies*, 2 (5): 624–653.

Bauman, Z. (2000). *Liquid Modernity*. Great Britain: Polity Press.

Beck, U. and Beck-Gernsheim, E. (2001/2002). *Individualization*. London: Sage.

Becker, G. (2007). *Libertarian Paternalism: A Critique—BECKER*. The Becker-Posner Blog. Available at: www.becker-posner-blog.com/2007/01/libertarian-paternalism-a-critique–becker.html

Bentham, J.-B. (1843). *The Works of Jeremy Bentham: Now First Collected*. J. Bowring (Ed.). Vol. 4. London: Snipkin, Marshall & Co.

Brasset, J. and Holmes, C. (2016). Building resilient finance? Uncertainty, complexity, and resistance. *The British Journal of Politics and International Relations*, 18 (2): 370–388.

Brunon-Ernst, A. (2016). Nudges and the limits of appropriate interference: Reading backwards from J.S. Mill's harm principle to Jeremy Bentham's indirect legislation. pp. 53–69.

Cromby, J. and Willis, M. E. H. (2014). Nudging into subjectification: Governmentality and psychometrics. *Critical Social Policy*, 34 (2): 241–259.

Dean, M. (1995). Governing the unemployed self in an active society. *Economy and Society*, 24 (4): 559–583.

Duménil, G. and Lévy, D. (2007) Finance and Management in the Dynamics of Social Change: Contrasting two trajectories - United States and France, in Assassi L., Nesvetailova A., Wigan D., (Eds.), *Global Finance in the New Century: Beyond Deregulation*, New York: Palgrave Macmillan. pp. 127–147.

The Economist. (2011). *The Great Unknown. Can Policymakers Fill the Gaps in Their Knowledge about the Financial System?*. Jan 13th, print edition. London: The Economist Newspaper Limited.

Elliot, A. and Urry, J. (2010). *Mobile Lives*. London: Routledge.

Farrell, H. and Shalizi, C. (2011). "Nudge" policies are another name for coersion. *New Scientist*.

Farrell, H. (2017). "Nudges" aren't good for democracy. Oct 16. Available at: www.vox.com/the-big-idea/2017/10/16/16481836/nudges-thaler-nobel-economics-prize-undemocratic-tool

Fitoussi, J.-P. (2005). New Social Norms and Economic Policies in Europe. *Reflets et perspectives de la vie économique*, XLIV (1): 61–65.

Foster, J. B. (2009). A failed system. The world crisis of capitalist globalization and its impact on China. *Monthly Review*, March.

Foucault, M. (1995) *Discipline and Punish: The Birth of the Prison*. New York: Vintage Books.

Foucault, M. (2004). *The Birth of Biopolitics: Lectures at the Collège de France 1978–1979*. G. Burchill (Trans.). London: Palgrave Macmillan.

Froud, J., Johal, S., Leaver, A., and Williams, K. (2006). *Financialization and Strategy: Narrative and Numbers*. London: Routledge.

Galič, M., Timan, T., and Koops, B.-J. (2017). Bentham, deleuze and beyond: An overview of surveillance theories from the panopticon to participation. *Philosophy & Technology*, 30 (1): 9–37.

Garland, D. (1996). The limits of the sovereign state: Strategies of crime control in contemporary society. The *British Journal of Criminology*, 36 (4) Autumn: 445–471.

Glaeser, E. L. (2004). Psychology and the market. *American Economic Review*, 94 (2): 408–413.

Halpern, D. (2015). *Inside the Nudge Unit: How Small Changes Can Make a Big Difference*. London: WH Allen.

Hobsbawm, E. (2007). *Globalisation, Democracy and Terrorism*. London: Abacus.

Hull, G. (2015). Successful failure: What Foucault can teach us about privacy self-management in a world of Facebook and big data. *Ethics and Information Technology*, 17 (2): 89–101.

International Labour Office. (2016). *Women at Work: Trends 2016*. Geneva: ILO.

Kahneman, D. (2011). *Thinking, Fast and Slow*. New York: Farrar, Straus and Giroux.

Kalleberg, A. and Vallas, S. (2018). Probing Precarious Work: Theory, Research, And Politics. In A. Kalleberg and S. Vallas (eds). *Precarious Work: Causes, Characteristics, and Consequences*. Bingley, UK: Emerald. pp. 1–30.

Keynes, J. M. (1936 (1964)). *The General Theory of Employment, Interest, and Money*. New York: Harcourt Brace.

Kitchin, R., Lauriault, T. P., and McArdle, G. (2017). *The Data and the City*. London: Routledge.

Klauser, F. R. and Albrechtslund, A. (2014). From self-tracking to smart urban infrastructures: Towards an interdisciplinary research agenda on big data. *Surveillance & Society*, 12 (2): 273–286.

Klick, J. (2010). The dangers of letting someone else decide. *The Cato Unbound. A Journal of Debate*. Response Essays, April 9. https://www.cato-unbound.org/2010/04/09/jonathan-klick/dangers-letting-someone-else-decide.

Kuttner, R. (2018). *Can Democracy Survive Global Capitalism?* New York: W.W. Norton.

Leeson, R. (2003). *Ideology and the International Economy: The Decline and Fall of Bretton Woods*. New York: Palgrave MacMillan.

Lima, G. and Madi, M. A. C. (Eds.). (2016). *Capital and Justice*. Bristol, UK: WEA Books.

Loewenstein, G. and Haisley, E. (2006). The economist as therapist: Methodological ramifications of "light" paternalism. In A. Caplin and A. Schotter (Eds.), *The Handbook of Economic Methodologies: Vol. 1. Perspectives on the Future of Economics: Positive and Normative Foundations*. Oxford: Oxford University Press. pp. 210–245.

Madi, M. A. C. (2018). Pension funds' challenges after the 2008 global crisis: Key problems for future generations. *The Open Journal of Economics and Finance*, 2: 117–125.

Malik, S. (2013). Joobseekers made to carry our bogus psychometric tests. *The Guardian*, 30 April.

Manokha, I. (2018). Surveillance, panopticism, and self-discipline in the digital age. *Surveillance & Society*, 16 (2): 219–237.

McGuigan, J. (2014). The neoliberal self. *Culture Unbound*, 6: 223–240.

Mettler, S. (2009). Promoting inequality: The politics of higher education policy in an era of conservative governnance. In L. Jacobs and D. King (Eds.), *The Unsustainable American State*. New York: Oxford University Press. pp. 197–222.

Mill, J. S. (1859 (2011)). *On Liberty*. The Project Gutenberg. EBook. #34901. London: The Walter Scott Publishing Co.

Monohan, T. (2017). Regulating belonging: Surveillance, inequality, and the cultural production of abjection. *Journal of Cultural Economy*, 10 (2): 191–206.

Oakeshott, M. (1991). *Rationalism in Politics and Other Essays*. Indianapolis: Liberty Press.

OECD (2009). *OECD Private Pensions Outlook 2008*. France: OECD Publishing.

OECD (2015). *OECD Regulatory Policy Outlook 2015*. Paris: OECD Publishing.

OECD (2018) *OECD Pensions Outlook 2018*. France: OECD Publishing.

Orwell, G. (1949) *1984*. London: Secker and Warburg.

Packard, V. (1957). *The Hidden Persuaders*. New York: David McKay, Inc.

Polanyi, K. (1944 (1971)). *The Great Transformation*. 11th edn. Boston, MA: Beacon Press.

Polanyi-Levitt, K. (2013). *From the Great Transformation to the Great Financialization*. London: Zed Books.

Polivka, A. and Nardone, T. (1989). On the definition of "contingent work". *Monthly Labor Review*. December: 9–16.

Pykett, J., Jones, R., Welsh, M., and Whitehead, M. (2014). The art of choosing and the politics of social marketing. *Policy Studies*, 35 (2): 97–114.

Pyysiäinen, J., Halpin, D., and Guilfoyle, A. (2017). Neoliberal governance and "responsibilization" of agents: Reassessing the mechanisms of responsibility-shift in neoliberal discursive environments. *Distinktion: Journal of Social Theory*, 18 (2): 215–235.

Ramsay, I. (2012). *Consumer Law and Policy: Text and Materials on Regulating Consumer Markets*. Oxford, UK: Bloomsbury Publishing.

Rizzo, M. J. and Whitman, D. G. (2007). Paternalist slopes. *NYU Journal of Law & Liberty*, 2 (3): 411–443.

Rizzo, M. J. and Whitman, D. G. (2009b). The knowledge problem of new paternalism. *BYU Law Review* 2009 (4): 905–965.

Rizzo, M. J. and Whitman, D. G. (2009a). Little brother is watching you: New paternalism on the slippery slopes. *Arizona Law Review*, 51: 685–739.

Saint-Paul, J. (2011). *The Tyranny of Utility: Behavioral Social Science and the Role of Paternalism*. Princeton, NJ: Princeton University Press.

Scherrer, H. (2006). The inhumanity of governemtn burieaucracies. In R. Higgs and C. Close (Eds.), *The Challenge of Liberty: Classical Liberalism Today*. Oakland, CA: The Independent Institute. pp. 199–214.

Standing, G. (2011). *The Precariat: The New Dangerous Class*. London: Bloomsbury Academic.

Stiglitz, J. (2015) Of the 1%, by the 1%, for the 1%. *Vanity Fair Magazine*, 30 April 2011. Available at: www.vanityfair.com/news/2011/05/top-one-percent-201105

Stockhammer, E. (2009). The finance-dominated accumulation regime, income distribution and the present crisis. *Papeles de Europa*, 19 (2009): 58–81.

Stone, J. (2013). Why downing street psychologists lied to jobseekers. *The New Statesman*, 2 May.

Sunstein, C. (1996). Social norms and social roles. *Columbia Law Review*, 96 (4): 903–968.

Sunstein, C. (2015). The ethics of nudging. *Yale Journal on Regulation*, 32: 413–450.

Sunstein, C. (2016). *The Ethics of Influence: Government in the Age of Behavioral Science*. New York: Cambridge University Press.

Sunstein, C. and Thaler, R. (2003). Libertarian paternalism is not an oxymoron. *University of Chicago Law Review*, 70 (4): 1159–1202.

Thaler, R. and Sunstein, C. (2003). Libertarian paternalism. *The American Economic Review*, 93 (2): 175–179.

Thaler, R. H. and Sunstein, C. R. (2008). *Nudge: Improving Decisions about Health, Wealth, and Happiness*. New Haven, CT: Yale University Press.

White, M. (2013). *The Manipulation of Choice: Ethics and Libertarian Paternalism*. Washington DC: Cato Institute.

Whitman, G. (2010). My fears affirmed: *The Conversation. The Cato Unbond: Journal of Debate*. April 13. Available at: www.cato-unbound.org/2010/04/13/glen-whitman/fears-affirmed

Wichert, I. (2002). Job insecurity and work intensification: The effects on health and well-being. In B. Burchell, D. Lapido and F. Wilkinson (eds.) *Job Insecurity and Work Intensification*. London: Routlegde.

Yeung, K. (2012). Nudge as fudge. *Modern Law Review*, 75 (1): 122–148.

Zuboff, S. (2015). Big other: Surveillance capitalism and the prospects of an information civilization. *Journal of Information Technology*, 30 (1): 75–89.

Zuboff, S. (2019). Interview. Available at: https://news.harvard.edu/gazette/story/2019/03/harvard-professor-says-surveillance-capitalism-is-undermining-democracy/

Conclusion

Minds, markets, and economic policy in the neoliberal age

Behavioural economics aims to apply psychological research to current economic and social challenges. In the context of neoliberal governance, behavioural policy insights have become spread in policy agendas to help citizens make "better" (rational) choices. The proposal involves a new approach to governments, markets, and societies.

Behavioural economics addresses the idea of bounded rationality since real people suffer from a variety of cognitive biases, including lack of self-control, excessive optimism, status quo bias, and susceptibility to framing of decisions, among others. Against the rational *homo economicus*, Thaler and Sunstein consider many heuristics and biases that explain the gap between our good intentions and actual behaviour. Therefore, human behaviour and choice exhibit bounded rationality, bounded self-interest, and bounded willpower. What behavioural economics explores in economic decision-making is that people are vulnerable to framing effects. Then, nudges are "soft" government interventions that can help people act rationally and, according to, Thaler and Sunstein, the possibilities for nudges are everywhere.

In the last decade, mainly after the 2008 global financial crisis, the debate about the ethics of nudges, by warning about their intrusiveness and transparency, put in to question the definition of a "nudge" as well as the predictive power of the "sciences of human behaviour". Indeed, the debate calls for a reflection on the methods and evidence of behavioural scientists. Other voices also are sceptical about the euphoria surrounding the use of nudge-based solutions to addressing major public policy problems.

On the whole, the book highlights the relation between nudges and Libertarian Paternalism. To understand the relevance of the meaning of Libertarian Paternalism, the concept deserves attention in historical and philosophical perspectives. In this attempt, the classical libertarianism of

Hayek and the Libertarian Paternalism of Thaler and Sunstein were analysed. The Libertarian Paternalists perspective argues that the role of public policy is to improve the individual decision making since humans are predictably irrational in various ways. The use of nudges as government interventions aims to help people increase their welfare, something they cannot do by themselves due to cognitive biases. Libertarian Paternalism maximally preserves the freedom of choice while the government interventions frame choices, leaving the final decisions to individuals.

The Dark Side of Nudges addresses that it is time to reconsider how knowledge and power re-frame human behaviour as an object of governance. In this attempt, relevant topics have attracted interest and reflection. First, this book provides a critical evaluation of the epistemological assumptions underlying behaviourally-informed policies. Second, this book calls for a reflection on the normative theory of nudges that relies on a positivist research program centred on a particular conception of autonomy: individuals make free choices, but to act "normally" (rationally) they need help to avoid flaws in behaviour. Third, looking at nudges in their wider context, it is possible to identify broader trends in neoliberal governance which require more detailed analysis.

At the heart of the current concerns about the outcomes of the transformations in governmentality is the extent to which the science and technology of nudges is being applied and spread under the Libertarian Paternalism's discourse. While behavioural thinking fits in conceptually and methodologically with positive psychology, Foucault´s analysis on biopolitics opens up a reflection on neoliberal governmentality that situates nudging in a wider theoretical and historical perspective.

Indeed, the global spread of nudges raises concerns as to whether economic policy should be built upon control trials and laboratory experiments, and which are the unexposed issues in these policy recommendations. The book argues that behavioural economics has not abandoned the Cartesian narrative and the ideal of rationality that have been deconstructed by Nietzsche and Foucault, among others, in the last centuries. Relying on Foucault's analysis on normalization in modern societies, this book proposed a reflection on the techniques of modern power that aim at defining what is normal (rational). In the contemporary scenario, individuals and populations are brought into conformity with the rational social norm. In doing so, such techniques of modern governmentality perpetuate the use of nudges as natural and necessary. A critical perspective toward Libertarian Paternalism enhances the understanding of the hidden forms of power and processes of subjectivation.

The Libertarian Paternalist´ discourse of (re-)framing highlights the individuals' desire for personal freedom and better quality of life. However, on behalf of their dual psychological system, there is a trade-off; that is to say, individuals sacrifice one of their selves in order to pursue rational choices. According to Thaler and Sunstein, there is no alternative to nudging people.

The Dark Side of Nudges calls for a reflection on the rationality and politics of neoliberalism in the age of behavioural economics. The neoliberal governance of self-care (or neoliberal governance of the self) relies on the explanation of Kahneman's functioning of the human brain that systematically deviate from rational decisions. While behavioural governance constitutes a distinctly mode of policy-making that comes with specific philosophical quandaries, we call for a reflection on the relation between the individual changes in subjectivity and the macro-changes in economics, politics, and society. Neoliberalism actually frames the meaning of everyday life. As well as promoting the self-regulated markets, neoliberalism is implicated in an ideological battle for promoting "rational minds".

In truth, the neoliberal transformations in market societies have shown that the modernization processes enhance further modifications in behaviours, values, and ideas. These changes could be understood taking into consideration the way in which the economy relates to social organization and culture and the impacts of economic and political institutions on human livelihoods. Shedding light on the contributions on Bentham´s Panopticon and Foucault's biopolitics, this book illuminates a vast set of effects of nudging citizens, on the control of life, and fosters further reflections on economic inequality, technocracy, surveillance, and the future of democracy. The nudge discourse relies on a governmental, unelected technocracy that may be able to exploit cognitive biases and heuristic strategies in order to nudge people. The threatening of the use of manipulative strategies and the unseen capture of information may bypass the already unacceptable levels of social, economic, and political inequality.

Nudging citizens, as the neoliberal governance of the self, reveals the active role of governments in the so called self-regulated markets. Behind the systemic re-framing of the choice architecture, there is the belief of Libertarian Paternalists (and of the rationalism in politics) that political problems can be tackled as technical ones. While Libertarian Paternalists favour the government of experts, they argue that nudges free people to spend their time on shaping their real true preferences. What is hidden behind this celebration of free time to shape true preferences?

Relying on technocracy in order to have free time to spend on "real" true preferences enhances the depoliticization of decisions in the public sphere. Relying on the government technocracy, the Libertarian Paternalist state turns out to be an administrative state.

Then, underlying Libertarian Paternalism is the transformation of the state into an administrative machine that resolves political conflicts bureaucratically, as Roger Berkowitz (2019) recently warned when he recalled the analysis of Hannah Arendt (1972) on the crisis of representative democracies, and highlighted that the rise of technocratic bureaucracies reinforces the fact that politics is governed by experts. However, it does not mean that politics may be less tyrannical or despotic.

In this scenario, the spread of nudges as government tools designed by experts poses additional concerns for the current debate on surveillance and freedom, since social control is at the core of the neoliberal techniques of power.

Postmodern criticism has brought to light relevant discussions around some of the presuppositions of the Enlightenment tradition that highlights the role of scientific knowledge guiding the action of individuals. In postmodern culture, there has been a change in the status of knowledge. According to Jean François Lyotard (1979 (1984)) the new way of applying knowledge in postmodern societies reinforces the commodification of knowledge itself, that is, knowledge is and will be produced for sale. The outcomes of this practice can be clearly perceived in postmodern societies in the information war. Therefore, Lyotard warned that knowledge turns out to be nothing more than a powerful instrument of domination. Thus, the philosopher establishes an indissoluble relationship between knowledge and power in postmodern culture where knowledge has a pragmatic nature. In this setting, the scientific discourse in behavioural economics will only be valid if it is the result of experimentation in control trials. Then, nudging citizens is related to small-sized policy remedies on behalf of the scientific claims that individuals accept small changes to make rational decisions and be happy. *The Dark Side of Nudges* highlights that this scientific knowledge turns out to be isolated from society.

Without the reference to a transcendentalist belief that confers intelligibility and normativity to human actions, people's behaviours are nowadays guided by new myths. The spread of such myths, such as the laws of the self-regulated markets, not only reveals a fragmentation of knowledge but also a deep social fragmentation. In this setting, new processes of subjectivation and new ways of being in the world are overwhelmed by hedonistic behaviours. In the place of utopias, the target of individual wellbeing and happiness, based on utilitarian criteria, underlies the moral of post-modern Western societies. In truth, the rational and hedonistic way of life looks after individual welfare, that is to say, individual benefits derived from the consumption of good and services.

The ideology of economic liberalism supports the self-regulation of the markets as the only organizing principle in the economic sphere, that is to say, the powerful mechanism for the organization of human life. Current economic dynamics of self-regulated markets has been strengthening a concept of human existence that is crossed by the promise of rationality and the search for efficiency and productivity. Rationality, instead of serving the human purpose, closes in on itself to become its own finality. Indeed, such rationality is overwhelmed by unemployment, precarious work, social exclusion, and impoverishment. In addition to these trends, resource exhaustion and the threats against the environment also show deleterious outcomes of present-day forms of economic power.

In accordance to Polanyi´s theoretical contribution, a society is a living organism whose *ethos* is the result of a complex combination of customs, norms, attitudes, aspirations that shape institutions. Remembering the words of Polanyi in *The Great Transformation* (1944, 60):

> the control of the economic system by the market is of overwhelming consequence to the whole organization of society: it means no less than the running of society as an adjunct to the market. Instead of economy being embedded in social relations, social relations are embedded in the economic system. … society must be shaped in such a manner as to allow that system to function according to its own laws. This is the meaning of the familiar assertion that a market economy can function only in a market society.

The market economy dramatically impacts on the social sphere since the spread of rational and utilitarian values turns to desegregate social relationships and threaten the civilization from annihilation. Following a Polanyian perspective, we can claim that the rationality of nudges, as a "soft" government intervention, reveals that the economy is disembedded from society.

Another relevant conclusion is that the policy approach to nudging citizens needs to be apprehended in the context of rationalism in politics where the role of technocrats – and their knowledge – is crucial to achieve specific policy goals. Indeed, the rationality of nudges turns out to de-historicise government "best practices" from the economic and social context. As a result, social problems are conceptualized as issues of psychological pathology.

Then, while being designed by "neutral" experts, nudges as policy tools seem to be divorced from the actual political and social processes of norm-formation. Taking into account the results of control trials, the so-called behavioural best practices and policies aim to enhance changes in individual behaviours that should be accomplished in accordance with the neoliberal governance of the self. As a consequence, the nudge approach to policy-making turns out to neglect current economic and social challenges while favoring individual behavioural changes towards "being rational", self-optimization, well being, and happiness.

However, as Polanyi highlighted, so-called human rationality is not compatible with the goals of peace and freedom. Polanyi contended that the "iron" laws governing a competitive market economy are not human laws. At this respect, Polanyi (1944, 131) draws attention to the outcomes of the self-regulated markets:

> The true significance of the tormenting problem of poverty now stood revealed: economic society was subjected to laws which were not human laws.

He added that the so called human rationality is not compatible with the goals of peace and freedom. If people want peace and freedom, they must make choices about the aims of their societies (Polanyi 1944, 263). Indeed, his contribution opens up new perspectives to think about an ethical living in contemporary capitalism. If economic and social change is to be authentically community-oriented, it needs to make room for values and behaviours that favour social standing. An ideal of social justice can be summarized in the following words: "The economy has to serve society, not the other way around."

The current debate on minds, markets and policy making certainly provides new openings for (re)orienting the policy targets in order to favour job creation, income distribution, poverty reduction and social welfare, without neglecting the relevance of a gender perspective in social reproduction.

Looking back, the experience of the 1930s revealed that a deep crisis can result in very diverse ideological and institutional responses. Although crises create opportunities for progressive policy and institutional reforms, the outcomes depend on the alignment of social and political forces. Therefore, transformative social policies should be thought without neglecting political configurations, social actors, and movements.

In conclusion, what is needed is a deep and large political shift that can lead to "self-protection" in an otherwise market dominated society. In this attempt, individuals are called to rethink values and actions without neglecting the institutional paths that affect the life of the *polis*.

References

Arendt, H. (1972). *Crises of the Republic: Lying in Politics, Civil Disobedience on Violence, Thoughts on Politics, and Revolution*. New York: Harcourt Brace Jovanovich.

Berkowitz, R. (2019). The four prejudices underlying our crises of democracy. *HA: The Journal of the Hannah Arendt Center*, March 22. pp. 15–22.

Lyotard, J. F. (1979 (1984)). *The Postmodern Condition*. Manchester, UK: Manchester University Press.

Polanyi, K. (1944). *The Great Transformation: The Political and Economic Origins of Our Time*. New York: Rinehart.

Index

addictive behaviour 13
advertising industry 79
AJBT (as judged by themselves) criteria 18
anchoring-and-adjustment choice heuristic **12**
anomalies 58
anti-paternalism 31
Arendt, Hannah 98
Ariely, Dan 2
Arrow, Kenneth 8
austerity policies 73, 77, 79
Australia 3; pension assets 73
auto-enrolment in pension plans 36
automatic thinking 11, 90
availability bias 11
availability choice heuristic **12**

BASIC (Behaviour, Analysis, Strategies, Intervention, Change) project, OECD 39–40
Beck, Ulrich 76
Becker, Gary 83
Beck-Gernsheim, Elisabeth 76
Behaviour, Analysis, Strategies, Intervention, Change (BASIC) project, OECD 39–40
behavioural economics 7, 10, 16, 42, 70, 95, 98; development of 23; importance of 1–3; methodological issues 46–53; philosophical issues 53–58
behavioural insights (BI) 39–41
Behavioural Insights Team/BIT (Nudge Unit), UK 2–3, 18, 24, 36–37, 37–38, 49, 79, 80
behavioural interventions *see* nudges
"behavioural market failures" 14, 64
Bentham, Jeremy 84, 90, 97
Bentham, Samuel 84
Berkowitz, Roger 98
BI (behavioural insights) 39–41
Big Data 85, 86–90, 97
biopolitics 71–72, 85–86, 90, 96, 97
BIT/Behavioural Insights Team (Nudge Unit), UK 2–3, 18, 24, 36–37, 37–38, 49, 79, 80
Blair, Tony 38
bounded rationality 7, 10, 95
Brasset, James 86
Brunon-Ernst, Anne 84
bureaucracies 17, 34, 69, 70, 98
business practices 38

cafeteria manager example 30
Camerer, Colin 8
Cameron, David 24, 38
Canada 3; pension assets 73
Cartesian philosophy 54–55, 57, 59, 96
Cartwright, Nancy 50
central banks 26, 28, 77
Chicago School 10, 71
choice architecture 24, 36; cognitive biases in 53
choice determination 16
choice, freedom of 2, 33–36
choice heuristics **12**, 12–14

Cialdini, Robert 2
citizens 24–25, 38–39, 64, 68, 69, 79, 82, 84, 89–91, 95, 97, 98, 99
citizenship 26–27, 69; weakening of 89
classical behaviourism 7
classical liberalism 25–28, 41, 52, 69, 71, 95–96; *see also* liberalism
climate change 72
Coase, Ronald 10, 16
cogito 55, 57
cognitive biases 7, 8, 9–12, 13, 35, 58, 95, 97; in choice architecture 53
cognitive boundaries 35
"cognitive illusions" 11
cognitive psychology 7, 10
"cold" psychological states 13
commodification 89, 98
community safety 39
competition 26, 51
completeness 16
confirmation bias 12
consumer debt 77, 80
consumer preferences 18; *see also* freedom of choice
consumer rationality 10
consumer sovereignty 10
context-dependence 16, 47–50
context-dependence bias 12
context-independence 9, 16
control *see* discipline and control, and nudges
control trials 18, 46, 96; *see also* RCTs (randomized controlled trials)
"cool-off" periods 36
corporate strategies 5, 64, 90
cost-benefit analysis 14
cultural evolution 26

dark nudges 76–83
Darling, Matthew 53–54
DB (defined benefit)/DC (defined contribution) pension plans 73–74
Deaton, Angus 50
default rules 14–15, 24, 25, 31, 35–37, 53
democracy 82, 89, 97, 98
deregulation 64, 65, 70–71, 72, 76–77, 90
Descartes 54–55, 57, 59, 96
Devas, Stanton Charles 1
digital nudges 83–90
discipline and control 83–96
doers (type of *human*) 10
downsizing, corporate 75–76
DPT (Dual Process Cognitive Theories) 11, 72, 90

EAST (Easy, Attract, Social, Timely) 38
economic knowledge 3, 4, 53
econs 10, 90
education 39, 41; role of government in 34; surveillance practices in 88
efficient markets hypothesis 10
emotional factors in decision-making 1, 11, 13
employment: employability 74–76, 87; employment flexibility 74; and neoliberalism 75–76; precarious 74–75, 78–79; *see also* labour market flexibility; unemployment
endowment effect 14
ethics 32, 42, 68–69, 95; ethical challenges 82–83
excessive optimism 10, 95
experimental government 18, 49
experimental setup in behavioural economics 47–53
experts 31, 36, 69, 85, 97, 98
externalities 15
extremeness aversion 24

familiarity choice heuristic **12**
Farrell, Henry 83, 89-90
Ferguson, Adam 71
finance, surveillance practices in 88
financialization 64, 66, 67, 70, 80, 90
fiscal austerity 77, 79
Fitoussi, Jean-Paul 80
Foucault, Michel 57–58, 58–59, 71–72, 85–86, 90, 96, 97
framing 11, 18, 95; "default rule decision" frames 14–15
Frederick, Shane 12
freedom 27; as a goal 100; *see also* classical liberalism; liberalism
freedom of choice 2, 33–36
Freud, Sigmund 56
Friedman, Milton 33–35, 47–48
Friedman, Rose 33–35
Fullbrook, Edward 54

Gale, Harlow 79
gender wage gap 78
Germany 3; Ordoliberals 71
Gilson, Étienne 55
global business 82
global financial crisis 2008 67, 73, 77
globalization, and inequality 66–67
Google 89
government, experimental 18, 49
governmentality 85–86; transformations in 65–70, 96
governments: BI (behavioural interventions) 24; Friedman and Friedman's four duties of 33; role in economy and markets 25–28, 52; role in education 34; tools for managing social norms 17

Halpern, David 18, 36–37, 37–38, 49, 72, 79, 87
happiness 15–18, 68, 98
harm principle 32, 83
Hausman, Daniel M. 16
Hayek, Friedrich August von 25–28, 41, 51–52, 64, 83, 96
healthcare systems 39, 41, 69; best practices in 38; surveillance practices in 88
Heidle, Stefan 47
high-risk behaviours 36
high-skilled employment, and women 78
Hobsbawm, Eric 66–67
Holmes, Christopher 86
homo economicus ("economic man") 1, 2, 8, 14, 18, 26, 46, 55, 71, 95
"hot" psychological states 13
House of Lords Science and Technology Select Committee Inquiry on Behaviour Change, 2011 42
household debt 77, 80
Hulls, Gordon 88
humans 10, 14, 23, 33, 90
Hume, David 71
hyperbolic discounting 13, 36

individual responsibility 64–65, 71–72
inequality 97; and capitalism 66–67; and nudges 76–80
informal work, and women 78
information: knowledge problem 51–53; *see also* Big Data
International Monetary Fund 65
involuntary unemployment 75
irrational behaviour 9

job creation 71, 100
job flexibility 74
job insecurity *see* precarious employment
Jobcentres 38

Kahneman, Daniel 1–2, 8, 9, 10, 11, 12, 14, 37, 48, 58, 72, 90, 97
Kalleberg, Arne 75
Keynes, John Maynard 75, 80–81
Keynesian economics 27, 28, 51–52
Klick, Jonhathan 83
knowledge: Cartesian view of 54–55; commodification of 98; economic 3, 4, 53; scientific 56, 98; *see also* experts
knowledge problem 51–53
Kukathas, Chandran 25
Kuttner, Robert 82

labour market 86; best practices in 38; flexibility 74–75, 77–78, 82; reforms 73
labour unions 77, 82
laissez-faire approach 24, 29
Leonard, Thomas C. 46
Levitt, Steven D. 50
liberalism 25–28, 41, 52; *see also* classical liberalism
Libertarian Paternalism 3, 4–5, 15, 17, 18, 24–25, 41–42, 64, 67–70, 82, 83, 84, 90, 95–98; guidelines for practical implementation 30–31; information and incentives 33–37; normativity of 46–47; principles of 28–32
libertarianism 2
liberty 24, 68, 69, 71
life-cycle hypothesis 10
liquidity 80–81
List, John A. 50
Loewenstein, George 42–43
loss aversion 10
Lyotard, Jean François 98

mandatory information disclosures 36
mandatory pension plans 73
marketing industry 3, 79
markets: governments' role in 25–28, 52; self-regulated 34, 67, 70, 75, 89, 97, 98, 99–100
Marx, Karl 51
mathesis universalis 55
mergers and acquisitions 75, 80, 81, 87
methodological issues in behavioural economics 46–53
Mettler, Suzanne 89
Mill, John Stuart 83–84
MIND-SPACE (Messenger, Incentives, Norms, Defaults, Salience, Priming, Affect, Commitments, Ego) 38
minds 25, 97, 100
monetary policy 26, 27, 28, 52
money supply, control of 26, 27
Monsell, Liam 47
moral values 56

naive diversification choice heuristic **12**
nation states/nationalism 65–66
negative externalities 15
neoclassical economics 1, 7, 51, 53–54
neoliberalism 64–65, 90, 96, 97; and employment 75–76; and nudges 70–76, 90–91; and self-governance 70–72, 82, 90, 97; and transformations in governmentality 65–70, 96
Netherlands, the 3; pension assets 73
"new paternalism" 24; *see also* Libertarian Paternalism
New Zealand: pension system reform 72
Nietzsche, Freidrich 55–57, 59, 96
normal 58–59, 60, 85, 96
normalization 5, 58–59, 72, 86, 96
normative approach/normativity 3, 4–5, 8, 9, 11, 16, 18, 23, 29, 35–36, 39, 43, 46–47, 49, 50, 57, 58–59, 70, 74, 96, 98
norms 59; *see also* social norms
nudge continuum 37, 70
Nudge Unit (Behavioural Insights Team/BIT), UK 2–3, 18, 24, 36–37, 37–38, 49, 79, 80
nudgeocracy 89–90
nudges 24; and Big Data 86–90; dark 76–83; definition 2, 17, 24; digital 83–90; discipline and control 83–86; and employability 74–76; ethics and democracy 80–83; four conditions for implementation 31; guidelines for 14–15; and inequality 76–80; information and incentives 33–37; and neoliberalism 70–76; new frontiers for 38–41; and pension savings 72–74; purpose of 2–3, 15; Sunstein's four classes of 31; three categories of 17–18

Oakeshott, Michael 70
Obama, Barack 24
obesity 72
OECD (Organisation for Economic Co-operation and Development) 39–40, 41
opportunity cost 10
optimism: errors of 13; excessive 10, 95
opt-outs 14, 24, 25, 32, 68, 69
ordinal utility theory 16
Ordoliberals 71
Orwell, George 90–91

Packard, Vance 79
Panopticon 84–85, 90, 97
part-time employment, and women 78
paternalism 2, 24, 25, 29, 32, 53, 68; *see also* Libertarian Paternalism
pathology, psychological 99
peace, as a goal 100
pension savings 36, 72–74; default options 36
pessimism, errors of 13
Pigou, Arthur 15, 16
planners (type of *human*) 10
Polanyi, Karl 89, 99–100
Polanyi-Levitt, Kari 67
politics 71, 82, 97, 98; of nudges 86, 90; rationalism in 26, 65, 68–70, 99; *see also* biopolitics
positive externalities 15
positivist psychology 55–56
postmodernism 98

power: Foucault on 58–59; and surveillance 86
precarious employment 74–75, 78–79
preferences 8–9, 16, 17, 18, 30–31, 36, 49, 53, 65, 88, 90, 97
present bias 11
price stability 26
privacy, and digital surveillance 88
privatization 76–77
"prospect theory" 8
psychology 47; positivist 55–56

Qatar 3
quasi-mandatory pension plans 73

radical incrementalism principle 18
rational choice theory 1, 7, 16, 23, 58; limitations of 8–9
rationalism, in politics 68–70
rationality 53–58, 96, 97, 99, 100
RCTs (randomized controlled trials) 3, 47, 48, 49–50; *see also* control trials
realism 3, 47–48
reflective (rational) thinking 11, 90
representativeness choice heuristic **12**
responsibility, individual 64–65, 71–72
retirement savings *see* pension savings
risk aversion 13
Rizzo, Mario J. 13, 37, 53, 70
Robbins, Lionel 16

Saint-Paul, Gilles 46, 70
scientific knowledge 56, 98
Scott, Walter Dill 79
Scottish Enlightenment 25
self-control, lack of 7, 9–10, 13, 18, 36, 95
self-governance 70–72, 82, 90, 97
selfishness 7
self-regulated markets 34, 67, 70, 75, 89, 97, 98, 99–100
September 11, 2001 events 66, 89
services sector, and women 78
Simon, Herbert 7
"sin taxes" 36
slippery-slope risk 51, 68, 69, 70
small-change tolerance 33
Smith, Adam 25, 35, 71
Smith, Vernon L. 58
SNAP (Salience, Norms, Affect, Priming) 38
social inclusion 39
social norms 16–17, 68, 96
South Africa: BI (behavioural interventions) 24
Standing, G. 74
status quo 14, 33
status quo bias 12, 95
subsidies, Pigouvian 15, 16
sunk cost fallacy choice heuristic **12**
Sunstein, Cass 2, 3, 4, 8, 10, 11–12, 14, 16, 17, 18–19, 23, 24, 29–30, 31–32, 33, 35–36, 37, 41, 46, 64, 68–70, 72, 82, 89, 95, 96, 97
surveillance 83–90, 97, 98
sustainability 39
System 1/System2 thinking 11, 72, 90

tax compliance 37
tax system, best practices in 38
taxes, Pigouvian 15, 16
Taylor, Dianna 59
technocracy 5, 72, 83, 97
Thaler, Richard 2, 3, 4, 8, 10, 11–12, 14, 17, 18–19, 23, 24, 28–30, 31, 35–36, 37, 41, 46, 49, 64, 68–70, 72, 82, 89, 95, 96, 97
totalitarianism 90–91
trade unions 77, 82
transaction cost hypothesis 10
transitivity 9, 16
transportation problem 47–50
Tversky, Amos 1–2, 8, 9, 10, 11, 14, 48, 58

Ubel, Peter 42–43
unemployment 86; involuntary 75; and neoliberalism 75–76; and nudges 79–80; and women 78; *see also* employment
United States 3; BI (behavioural interventions) 24; erosion of economic freedom 33, 34; pension assets 73; pension system reform 72
unpaid work, by women 79
utilitarianism 84
utility maximization 1, 7

Vallas, Steven 75
Vining, Rutledge 47

wages: gender wage gap 78
"war against terror" 66
Watson, John 7
Weber, Elke 2
welfare economics 15; neoclassical approach to 8–9
welfare state 27; transformation of 67; *see also* austerity policies
well-being, science of 18
"what works" 18, 19, 38, 40, 49, 50
Whitman, Douglas Glen 13, 37, 53, 70
willpower, lack of 7, 9–10, 13, 18, 36, 95
women, and employment 78–79
World Bank 65
World Trade Organization 65

youth policy 39

Zuboff, Shoshana 89

For Product Safety Concerns and Information please contact our EU representative GPSR@taylorandfrancis.com
Taylor & Francis Verlag GmbH, Kaufingerstraße 24, 80331 München, Germany

www.ingramcontent.com/pod-product-compliance
Ingram Content Group UK Ltd.
Pitfield, Milton Keynes, MK11 3LW, UK
UKHW020939200926
475569UK00011B/13
* 9 7 8 1 1 3 8 3 3 8 6 2 3 *